Turning
Green Wood

Turning
Green Wood

Michael O'Donnell

THE GUILD OF MASTER CRAFTSMAN PUBLICATIONS

First published 2000 by
Guild of Master Craftsman Publications Ltd
Castle Place, 166 High Street,
Lewes, East Sussex BN7 1XU

Reprinted 2001, 2002, 2003, 2004, 2005, 2006, 2008, 2010, 2012, 2014, 2016

Photographs by Joanne Kaar and Michael O'Donnell
except where otherwise stated
Line drawings produced by Simon Rodway from
originals by Michael O'Donnell
Pencil sketches on pages 44–8 by Michael O'Donnell

ISBN: 978-1-86108-089-9

A catalogue record for this book is available from the
British Library.

Publisher: Jonathan Bailey
Production Manager: Jim Bulley
Managing Editor: Gerrie Purcell
Editor: Stephen Haynes
Managing Art Editor: Gilda Pacitti
Design: Fineline Studios
Front cover photograph: David Bradford
Back cover photography: Joanne Karr and
Michael O'Donnell

Set in Palatino and Lucida Sans

Colour origination by Viscan Graphics (Singapore)
Printed in China

Contents

Warning

Although woodturning is safer than many other activities involving machinery, all machine work is inherently dangerous unless suitable precautions are taken.

Do not use timber which may come apart on the lathe – beware of faults such as dead knots, splits, shakes, loose bark, etc.

Avoid loose clothing or hair which may catch in machinery. Protect your eyes and lungs against dust and flying debris by wearing goggles, dust mask or respirator as necessary, but invest in an efficient dust extractor as well.

Pay attention to electrical safety; in particular, do not use wet sanding or other techniques involving water unless your lathe is designed so that water cannot come into contact with the electrics.

Keep tools sharp; blunt tools are dangerous because they require more pressure and may behave unpredictably.

It is not safe to use a chainsaw without the protective clothing which is specially designed for this purpose, and attendance on a recognized training course is strongly recommended. Be aware that regulations governing chainsaw use are revised from time to time.

Do not work when your concentration is impaired by drugs, alcohol or fatigue.

The safety advice in this book is intended for your guidance, but cannot cover every eventuality: the safe use of machinery and tools is the responsibility of the user. If you are unhappy with a particular technique or procedure, do not use it – there is always another way.

Measurements

Although care has been taken to ensure that the metric measurements are true and accurate, they are only conversions from imperial; they have been rounded up or down to the nearest whole millimetre, or to the nearest convenient equivalent in cases where the imperial measurements themselves are only approximate. When following the projects, use either the metric or the imperial measurements; do not mix units.

Introduction

'Turning green wood' means turning fresh timber straight from the log without any previous processing. It brings the craftsman into contact with the tree in its natural environment while it is still living and growing, which is the starting point of a fascinating, exciting and rewarding craft. Green woodturning reveals the special natural qualities of timber, both visual and tactile: its warmth and durability, its colour and grain patterns, the contrast between heart and sapwood, the special figure from the crotch wood and burrs that are found in infinite variety in the timbers of the world. Green turning converts this raw material into beautiful, artistic, decorative and functional pieces through a very satisfying process.

Working 'green' is exciting, with scope for experimentation and development, particularly in the area of bowls and hollow vessels, which have been dominant in green turning over the past twenty years. A large proportion of gallery work is turned 'green', because craftsmen have found in this approach a particular freedom of expression and design, with control over all aspects of the making process, and the ability to make full use of the natural features of the tree in each individual piece. The size of the tree and the turner's ability to handle it are the only limitations. Many pieces are made in one operation, after which the drying process is allowed to create the final shape. Other pieces – such as salad bowls, fruit bowls, sugar bowls or any kind of bowl which needs to be round when finished – are made by using the part-turning process, where the wood is initially turned in a green state, and the final turning is done when it has been dried. This combines the advantages of turning 'green' with those of using kiln-dried wood. It is ideal for work on a production basis, where a stock of part-turned bowls is built up and then worked through when dry, the turner replenishing the stock at the same time.

The green turning process itself is very attractive, because fresh wood cuts cleanly and easily and produces long ribbons of shavings, which reduces the time taken to rough out the pieces. Costs are also reduced, because timber in the log is cheaper than processed timber; sometimes the turner is even paid to remove unwanted trees.

From the conservation point of view, green turning makes good use of the home-grown timbers around us which have no commercial value, and of which there is an abundant supply that would otherwise be burnt as firewood or left to rot where it was cut or dumped. This means that our supply is no longer from the exotic rainforest and other tropical forests, the exploitation of which is destroying them.

The woodturner's basic knowledge of wood is fundamental to that all-important first step – assessing the potential of the tree as a source of bowls and vessels. Before investigating the inside of a tree – a destructive process – it is important to gather as much information as possible from its outside features. The bark and leaves provide clues as to the species, and whether it is hardwood or softwood. From this you will know something of the structure and colour of the wood. The leaf development and time of year will give you an indication of activity within the cambium layer between the bark and the wood, where the new wood is generated. Each mark on the bark gives an indication of what lies beneath. **Healing growth** shows where the surface has been damaged or a branch broken off. The wood between a branch and the main trunk above the pith is known as the **crotch** and contains decorative figured wood, the extent of which is seen in representative markings on the bark. Areas with **ripple** in the wood are also reflected in the bark pattern. The tree's growing environment will tell you something about its rate of growth, and therefore the spacing of the growth rings, if any. Its size will tell you how much useful wood there is.

However, green turning is a process which can be unpredictable for the uninitiated: the wood dries, shrinks, deforms, discolours and splits – all of which can happen at any stage of the process, from the harvesting to the final drying. These are a function of the natural properties of the wood, and anticipating these properties requires an understanding of the process of green turning. The object of this book is to guide you through the complete process, from harvesting to finished products – to teach you how to work *with* the wood, and make use of its many characteristics and features.

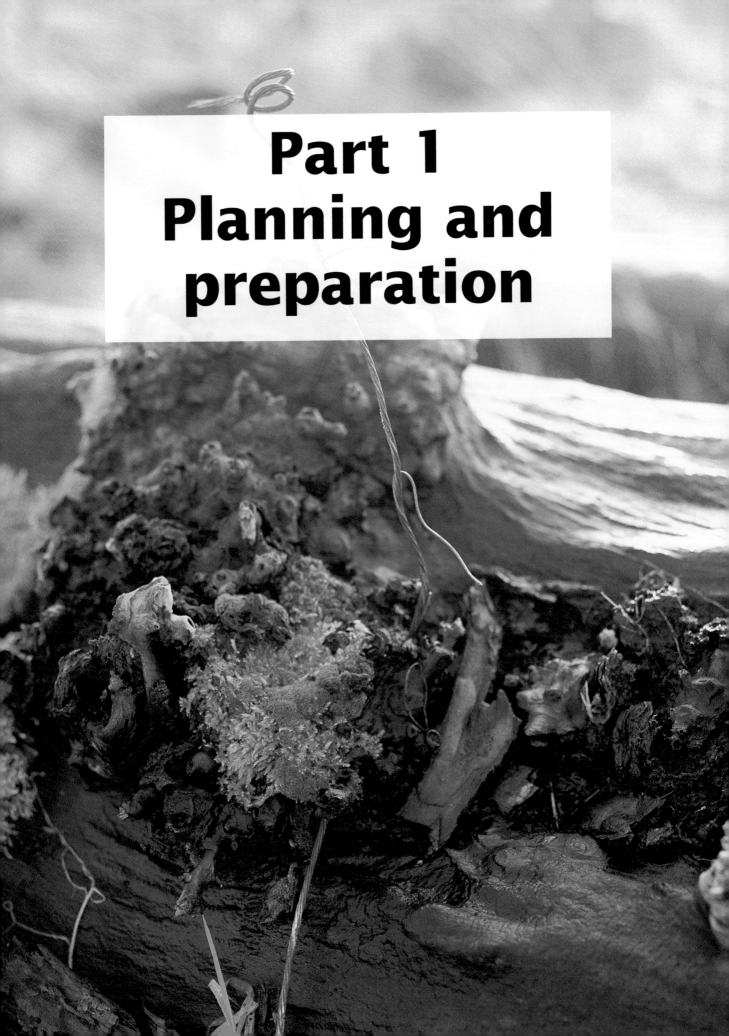

Part 1
Planning and preparation

1 The tree

Trees

The diversity of trees is immense. There are over 20,000 species of hardwood trees and around 600 species of softwood; these are used to produce commodities such as timber, cork, rubber, maple syrup, fruit and tea. Without them we would have a more primitive lifestyle – or we might not be here at all, because they provide much of the oxygen we need for life.

There are two main classifications of tree: **hardwood** and **softwood**. The terms have nothing to do with the physical hardness or strength of the wood, but refer to botanical differences. Hardwood trees have broad leaves, are usually deciduous, and bear a seed which is contained in a shell or fruit. Softwoods are mainly evergreen, have needle-like leaves, and produce an open, unprotected seed, usually contained in a cone. Although many temperate countries have a mixture of hardwoods and softwoods, their natural habitats are different: softwoods are hardy and prefer cooler climates, while hardwoods prefer temperate-to-tropical growing conditions.

Life cycle

Being living organisms, trees need food in order to thrive and grow. They have a food cycle which starts with taking in water and mineral nutrients from the ground through their roots, then transporting them up the tree, through the **sapwood**, to the leaves. Here the minerals and water are combined, by photosynthesis, with the sun's rays and carbon dioxide from the air to produce soluble carbohydrates and oxygen. The oxygen is given back to the atmosphere and approximately 90% of the water is given off through evaporation. The remaining carbohydrates, which are the nutrients for the tree in the form of sucrose sugars, are then transported back down the tree with the remaining water, through the inner bark (**outer phloem tissue**). This is then used to provide energy for the life of the tree, and for the production of new wood in the **cambium layer**; and some of it is stored in the **medullary rays** for future use.

In temperate climates growth is seasonal, and starts in the spring as the new leaves are formed. The cambium layer, which is a single-cell layer situated between the bark and the sapwood, divides to produce new sapwood on the inside and new bark on the outside, and this continues until the end of the growing season in autumn (Fig 1.1). But there are differences in structure and colour between the wood which is produced in spring, known as **early wood**, and the wood produced later in the season, known as **late wood**; and this gives rise to the distinctive **annual growth rings**. The width of the growth ring gives an indication of the growing conditions each year: periods of drought produce little growth or none at all, while good growing seasons produce a lot of growth and a wider ring. These annual changes produce a form of climatic 'fingerprint', which is the same for trees subject to the same conditions and can be used to date old wooden structures (this

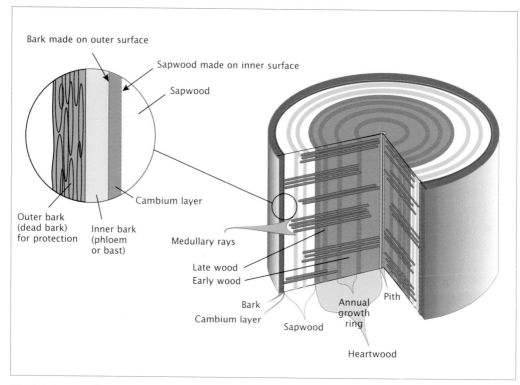

Fig 1.1 Section of a tree trunk, and detail showing the cambium layer where new growth occurs

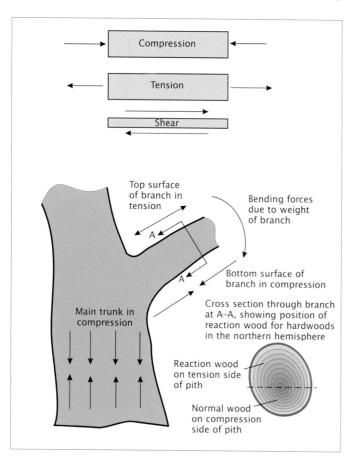

Fig 1.2 Stresses acting on the growing tree (in static conditions)

is known as **dendrochronology**). Growth rings are less obvious in trees grown in tropical conditions, where growth is continuous all year round.

As the tree grows, not all of the timber is required for food transportation, so the older sapwood becomes **heartwood**, which is then used for the storage of waste products. This process is often accompanied by a change in colour from the normal white or creamy-coloured sapwood of most trees to a darker heartwood.

Reaction wood

In static conditions, the main trunk of the tree is in compression from the weight of the tree, which is the normal stress that the tree structure is designed to withstand. Branches, not being vertical but sticking out sideways from the main trunk, create a new set of stresses through the bending moment caused by the weight of the branch. This puts the top of the branch in tension and the bottom part of the branch in compression. To withstand these stresses the tree builds what is known as **reaction wood** (Figs 1.2 and 1.3).

Hardwood trees in the northern hemisphere build the reaction wood on the tension side of the pith, which gives rise to the growth rings in branches being wider on the tension side (the upper side) than on the compression side. In the southern hemisphere this is reversed: hardwoods build the reaction wood on the compression side of the pith (the underside of the branch). Softwood trees on the other hand produce reaction wood on the opposite side of the pith to hardwoods in both northern and southern hemispheres.

Leaning trees have the same stresses as branches, and build the same reaction wood. Even vertical trunks with heavier branches on one side than the other will contain some reaction wood.

Reaction wood is different in structure and chemical composition from normal wood, and has very different properties. Shrinkage, particularly in the longitudinal direction, can be 20 times greater than in normal wood, and machinability is greatly reduced. The reaction wood element is one of the major reasons why the timber industry avoids limb wood. But, even with these characteristics, turners can use timber with reaction wood effectively.

Wood and moisture

When the tree is growing it contains vast amounts of moisture, called **sap**, which can weigh more than the wood itself. This moisture, which holds the minerals and nutrients, is transported around the tree through the cell structure. The standard measurement of the amount of moisture in the wood, the **moisture content (MC)**, is the ratio of the weight of moisture in the tree to the oven-dry

Fig 1.3 Sycamore from the northern hemisphere, showing the pith thrown off centre by a large area of reaction wood

weight of the wood, and is given as a percentage:

$$\frac{\text{weight of moisture in the tree}}{\text{oven-dry weight of tree}} \times \frac{100}{1} = \% \text{ MC}$$

or:

$$\frac{\text{weight of tree} - \text{oven-dry weight of tree}}{\text{oven-dry weight of tree}} \times \frac{100}{1} = \% \text{ MC}$$

The **oven-dry weight** is the weight of the wood with a zero moisture content. It is called the oven-dry weight because zero moisture content is obtained by drying in an oven at 103°C (217°F) until the weight becomes constant.

Moisture within the tree is regarded as being held in two ways (Fig 1.4). The first is known as **free moisture**, which is moisture contained within the cells, like water contained in a bucket. The second, known as **bound moisture**, is moisture contained within the fibre of the cell walls. When there is no free moisture and the cell walls are saturated with moisture, this is known as the **fibre saturation point (FSP)**. The moisture content at the fibre saturation point varies with the species, but is on average 30%.

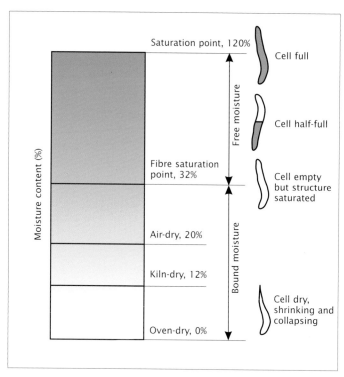

Fig 1.4 How moisture is held in the tree. The figures given are average ones, and do not represent a particular wood

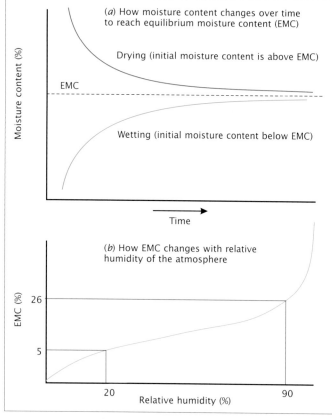

Fig 1.5 Wood and moisture

Equilibrium moisture content (EMC)

Once the tree has been harvested and slabbed, if it is then left in the atmosphere sheltered from the rain, it will begin to lose moisture to the atmosphere and become dryer. The amount it loses to the atmosphere is dependent on the local conditions of temperature and **relative humidity**. (Relative humidity is the ratio of the amount of water actually in the air at a particular temperature to the maximum amount of water it *could* hold at that temperature.)

The wood continues to lose moisture until it reaches a moisture-content level at which the drying stops. At this point the wood is in equilibrium with the atmospheric conditions of temperature and relative humidity. This condition is known as the **equilibrium moisture content (EMC)**. Every timber has a different EMC at any given temperature and humidity level. At 90% relative humidity and a temperature of 70°F (21°C), the average EMC for an average timber is 20% MC; while at 60% relative humidity and 70°F, the average EMC is 12.5%. The air-drying process is controlled by the relative humidity and temperature of the atmosphere.

Conversely, a very dry piece of wood, which has a moisture content below the EMC, will take in moisture from the atmosphere until it approaches the EMC. These two situations are shown in Fig 1.5*a*. The effect of humidity on EMC is shown in Fig 1.5*b*. The effect of temperature on EMC is small in comparison: EMC changes only about 1% for every 25°F (14°C) change from a datum of 70°F (21°C).

Shrinkage

Removal of moisture from the felled tree to levels below the fibre saturation point causes the wood to shrink. If we look at a simplified model of the 'average' tree structure we can see how the individual cells shrink, and what effect this has on the overall structure.

An individual cell will shrink when it dries (Fig 1.6*a*); the diameter shrinks on average 8%, while the length stays the same. If all the cells were orientated longitudinally in the tree, then the overall shrinkage of the tree would be the same as that of the individual cells – diameter and circumference 8%, length 0% – and the tree would be in equilibrium without internal stresses (Fig 1.6*b*). But in nature some of the cells are orientated radially from the pith (medullary rays), and this complicates the shrinkage of the tree (Fig 1.6*c*). The shrinkage around the circumference of the tree would be the same as the cell diameter shrinkage: 8%. In the radial direction there is conflict between the *longitudinal* shrinkage of the radial cells and the *diameter* shrinkage of the vertical cells. The resultant shrinkage of 4% is in the radial direction. Although the circumferential shrinkage is in equilibrium, there are internal stresses set up between the vertical and radial cells in the radial direction. The effect of the rays on the longitudinal shrinkage is very small (bringing it to 0.1%), but they also create internal stresses in the longitudinal direction (Fig 1.6*d*).

Standard shrinkages are measured, in the three dimensions of length, radius and circumference, from the wood's fibre saturation point dimension to either:

(*a*) the oven-dry condition of 0% moisture content (the general standard measurement in academic use)

or:

(*b*) 12% moisture content (used as the datum by the Building Research Establishment in the UK as a practical lower-level moisture content).

Shrinkage figures for individual species are given in Table 1. Remember that:

- **Longitudinal shrinkage** is shrinkage along the length of the grain. This is usually very small, with an average of around 0.1%, and throughout this book we ignore it as being insignificant.
- **Radial shrinkage** is shrinkage along radial lines out from the pith. This is much larger and averages around 4%.
- **Circumferential (or tangential) shrinkage** is shrinkage around the annual growth rings, and is the largest of all at an average of 8%.
- The **ratio** between the radial and circumferential shrinkages on average is 2:1.

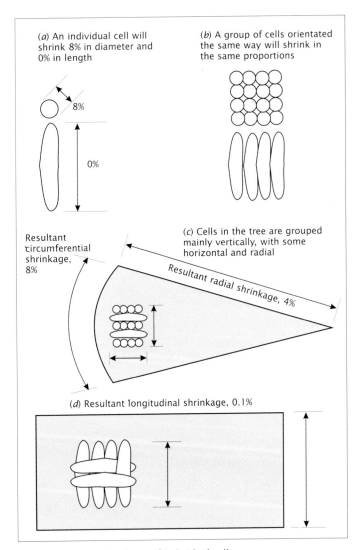

(*a*) An individual cell will shrink 8% in diameter and 0% in length

(*b*) A group of cells orientated the same way will shrink in the same proportions

Resultant circumferential shrinkage, 8%

(*c*) Cells in the tree are grouped mainly vertically, with some horizontal and radial

Resultant radial shrinkage, 4%

(*d*) Resultant longitudinal shrinkage, 0.1%

Fig 1.6 How the shrinkage of individual cells determines the overall shrinkage within the tree

Table 1: Average shrinkages, fibre saturation point to 0% MC (oven-dry) and 12% MC

Timber	Shrinkage					
	FSP to 12% MC			FSP to oven-dry		
	Radial (%)	Circumferential (%)	Ratio	Radial (%)	Circumferential (%)	Ratio
Hardwoods						
Ash, European *Fraxinus excelsior*	4.5	7.0	1.55			
Birch, European *Betula pubescens* and *B. pendula* (syn. *verrucosa*)	5.0	8.0	1.6			
Blackwood, Australian *Acacia melanoxylon*	5.0					
Cherry, European *Prunus avium*	3.5	6.5	1.9			
Dogwood, flowering *Cornus florida*				7.4	11.8	1.6
Elm, English and Dutch *Ulmus procera* and *U. hollandica*	4.5	6.5				
Elm, rock *U. racemosa*				4.8	8.1	1.7
Holly, American *Ilex opaca*				4.8	9.9	2.1
Holly, European *I. aquifolium*	5.0	12.0	2.4			
Jarrah *Eucalyptus marginata*	5.0	8.0	1.6			
Karri *Eucalyptus diversicolor*	5.0	10.0	2.0			
Madrone, Pacific *Arbutus menziesii*				5.6	12.4	2.2
Maple, red *Acer rubrum*				4.0	8.2	2.1
Maple, rock (sugar maple) *A. saccharum*	2.5	5.0	2.0			
Oak, American white *Quercus alba, Q. prinus, Q. lyrata, Q. michauxii*	3.0	5.5	1.85	5.6	10.5	1.85
Oak, European *Q. robur* (syn. *pedunculata*), *Q. petraea* (syn. *sessiliflora*)	4.0	7.5	1.9			
Purpleheart or **amaranth** *Peltogyne spp.*	2.0	4.5	2.25			
Queensland walnut *Flindersia brayleyana, F. pimentliana*	4.0	6.5	1.6			
Silver beech *Nothofagus menziesii*	3.0	6.0	2.0			
Sycamore, European *Acer pseudoplatanus*	2.5	5.5	2.2			
Tasmanian oak *Eucalyptus delegatenis, E. obliqua, E. regnans*	5.0	10.0	2.0			
Walnut, American *Juglans nigra*	2.5	3.5	1.4	5.5	7.8	1.4
Walnut, European *J. regia*	3.0	5.5	1.8			
Softwoods						
Kauri, Queensland *Agathis robusta, A. palmerstonii, A. microstachya*	2.2	3.5	1.6			
Pine, Monterey *Pinus radiata* (syn. *insignis*)	2.5	4.0	1.6			
Yew *Taxus baccata*	2.0	3.5	1.75			

Sources

Dept of the Environment, *Handbook of Hardwoods, Handbook of Softwoods*; Hoadley, *Understanding Wood* (see Select Bibliography on page 129)

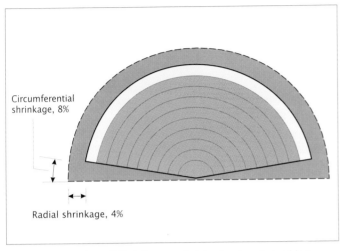

Fig 1.7 Shrinkage and distortion in a halved log

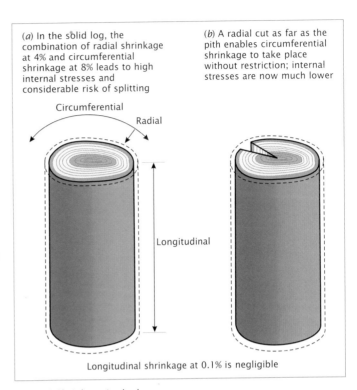

(*a*) In the solid log, the combination of radial shrinkage at 4% and circumferential shrinkage at 8% leads to high internal stresses and considerable risk of splitting

(*b*) A radial cut as far as the pith enables circumferential shrinkage to take place without restriction; internal stresses are now much lower

Circumferential

Radial

Longitudinal

Longitudinal shrinkage at 0.1% is negligible

Fig 1.8 Shrinkage in the log

The shrinkage values in the table are for 'normal' heartwood of the species. Shrinkage of other parts of the tree is often very different. Sapwood shrinks more than heartwood, particularly where there is a colour difference. Juvenile wood, which is the wood within the first few growth rings around the pith, shrinks less than the rest of the heartwood; this shows up in pieces which include the pith. Reaction wood has a very different structure to normal wood and tends to react more severely to drying: for example, longitudinal shrinkage can increase to 2%, which is 20 times the 'normal' amount. Figured wood, such as that from the crotch areas, burrs, etc., also shrinks differently.

Distortion

Distortion with drying is inevitable with any wood, as the shrinkages are different in each direction. This can be shown by looking at the change in shape of an average straight-grained log at the fibre saturation point which has been halved across the pith, then dried slowly and evenly to oven-dry (Fig 1.7). The length shrinks 0.1%, which will hardly be perceptible. The radius shrinks 4%, while the circumference shrinks 8%. This causes the two faces on either side of the pith (at 3 o'clock and 9 o'clock) to move towards 12 o'clock.

If the wood is dried in the round, the amount of circumferential shrinkage that can take place is restricted to the same percentage as the radial shrinkage, and this will create high internal stresses (Fig 1.8*a*). If the same log is cut lengthwise as far as the pith and then dried, the full circumferential shrinkage can take place, with fewer internal stresses (Fig 1.8*b*).

Stress and splitting

When the wood is dried quickly and unevenly, additional stresses are created during the drying process because the drying outer parts want to shrink while the wet inner parts do not. For example, the moisture will be lost very quickly from the cut end of a log while the centre remains unchanged. High stresses within the wood, however created, can cause either cracking on the surface of the timber or internal cell damage which reduces the strength of the wood and makes it more brittle. Careful storage and monitoring of the drying process will minimize these problems.

2 Bowls in the tree

Grain patterns

As the tree stands growing in the ground it is full of bowls and vessels of all shapes, sizes, colours and grain patterns – they are there for the taking (Fig 2.1). Cut a piece of the tree and turn away all the wood that isn't a bowl, and there you are. But which bowl did you get, and is it the one you wanted? With some care and planning you can get exactly what you want. Choosing the right grain pattern, colour contrast and edge shapes can make the difference between an average bowl and a great one.

The grain structure and growth rings of the tree provide wood with one of its most endearing characteristics: its grain pattern. Bowls are ideal shapes to explore the potential beauty of grain patterns, which are revealed in different forms depending on how the bowls are orientated in the tree. Being able to predict grain pattern is vital to successful bowl design.

Cross-grain bowls

A cross-grain bowl is one where the grain runs across the bowl from side to side, parallel to the base. This grain orientation is traditional in most of Europe, America and Australia.

Looking at Fig 2.2, you will see that I have drawn two bowls on the end of a log: they are the same shape, height and diameter, but positioned differently. The base of bowl A is close to the pith, while bowl B has its rim close to the pith. Although they have the same growth rings running through them, the grain patterns within the bowls are different. Bowl A has concentric oval shapes radiating out from the centre, while on bowl B there is a semicircular grain pattern radiating from the pith on both the near and far sides of the rim. This will show in plan view as two semicircular areas, with a different pattern across the

Fig 2.1 Bowls in the tree: the grain pattern, colour and final shape of each bowl will be determined by its position and orientation within the tree

centre where the two grain patterns merge, which will vary with the depth of the bowl.

Bowl C produces a third grain pattern. Looking into the bowl, the grain lines are almost straight, with a very slight curve away from the pith.

The three bowls described above show the three basic grain patterns you encounter in making cross-grain bowls from a straight-grained log; from these, the grain pattern for any other cross-grain bowl can be predicted.

End-grain bowls

An end-grain bowl is one which is in the upright position within the tree as it grows, so that the grain runs vertically through it. Bowls of this kind are traditional in Scandinavia, where softwoods and small hardwood species like birch are the most abundant raw materials. Working with end grain, bowls the same size as the tree trunk are convenient to make.

In Fig 2.3 I have drawn two end-grain bowls within the tree on the end of the log. Bowl D is centred away from the pith, and the other, bowl E, is centred on the pith. Looking into bowl D, you see curved lines, the radius of which gets smaller as they get closer to the pith. Looking into the second bowl, with the pith in the centre, you see the growth rings as they are in the tree. Any end-grain bowl has a grain pattern which is some combination of the above two.

We now have five basic grain patterns for cross-grain and end-grain bowls, from which the grain pattern of any bowl in a straight log with a straight

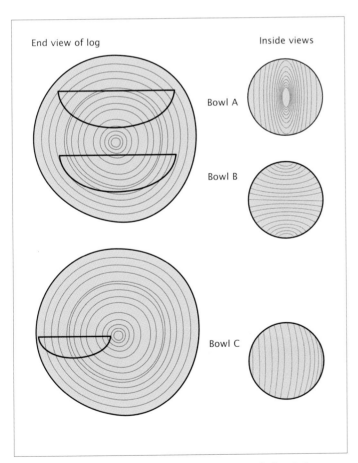

Fig 2.2 Grain patterns: cross-grain bowls in various orientations

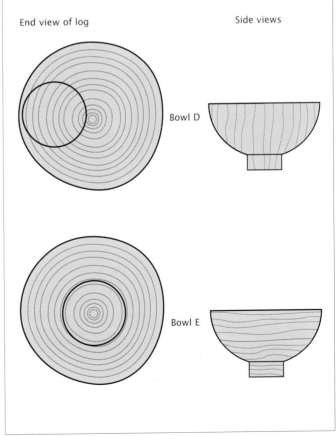

Fig 2.3 Grain patterns: end-grain bowls

grain, no matter how it is orientated in the tree, can be predicted.

Grain and colour

In addition to their grain patterns, many trees have a rich, dark heartwood of varied colours, surrounded by a contrasting creamy-white sapwood, and this contrast gives additional possibilities for bowl design.

Looking at the first log from which we cut bowls A and B, add in the heartwood colour, then transfer the heartwood area to the plan views of the bowls to see where it appears (Fig 2.4). On bowl A the heartwood is in an oval patch in the bottom; a larger area of heartwood would leave an undulating rim of sapwood around the edge. On bowl B the heartwood appears in semicircular patches at either side of the bowl. If the bowl shape is close to concentric with the growth rings, then as the heartwood is extended the sapwood becomes a stripe across the centre of the bowl – an attractive feature. In bowl C, half is dark heartwood with the other half light sapwood, and the divide is a straight line down the middle. Depending on the extent of the heartwood, end-grain bowl D could either be all sapwood, or part heartwood and part sapwood, divided vertically along one of the growth rings (Fig 2.5). Bowl E has a patch of heartwood in the bottom with the sides sapwood.

By drawing a few bowls on the end of a log we can envisage what the grain pattern and the colours of each bowl will be. This is an important step in the design

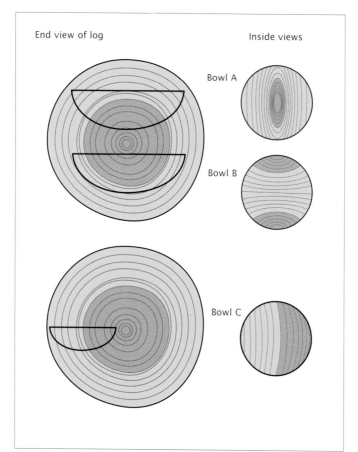

Fig 2.4 Grain and colour: cross-grain bowls in various orientations

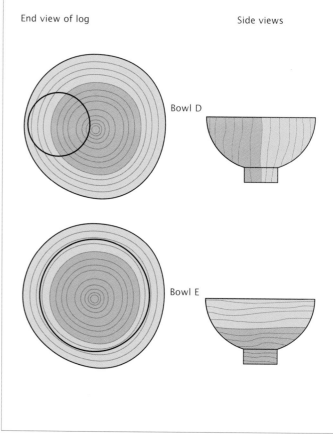

Fig 2.5 Grain and colour: end-grain bowls

process. To finish this section, I have drawn on the end of a log of tulipwood – the first tree I bought whole – a favourite type of bowl I was making in the early 1980s (Fig 2.6). Fig 2.7 shows a finished piece, with a sapwood rim and heartwood body.

Figure

As well as the regular growth rings there is another interesting aspect of the grain to explore, called **figure**. This denotes various kinds of irregular grain pattern which occur as part of the natural process of growing.

Crotch wood

Dramatic figure may be found in the crotch area between the main trunk and the branch. All the figure lies between the piths of the trunk and branch, in an area roughly conical in shape, running to a point where the two piths join. Feathery sections, the extent of which is usually indicated on the bark, run out radially to the surface. These surface markings are more obvious on smooth-barked trees (Fig 2.8). The length of figure is dependent on the angle of the branch to

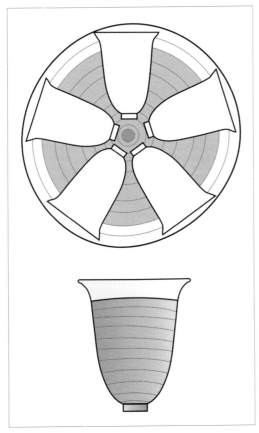

Fig 2.6 Tulipwood bowls in the log: an example of bowl A

Fig 2.7 One of the tulipwood vessels shown in the previous figure

Fig 2.8 Surface markings on the bark indicating presence of crotch figure

the tree (Fig 2.9). On branches square to the tree it is short; reducing the angle increases the length of the figure. When the angle is below 30° there tends to be a significant amount of bark inclusion, which reduces the usable amount of figure, but this also shows on the surface.

Careful planning is necessary to get the best out of this figure, right from harvesting, which is a critical point. The amount of figure in small trees, 6in (150mm) diameter or under, is not worth the effort, while over 20in (510mm) diameter is difficult to handle because of its size and weight. Logs between 10 and 15in (250 and 380mm) diameter are easier to handle and are therefore good sizes to start with. In a tree of this size it is best to go for one good bowl from the crotch area rather than two mediocre bowls, as much of the figure will otherwise be lost to the chainsaw.

Different bowl orientations in the crotch will each produce something different. In Fig 2.10 there are two cross-grain options, F and G, with a third example, H, made into the shape of a tall end-grain vessel containing much of the figure. Bowl I is a natural-edge bowl incorporating the crotch wood as well as an interesting rim with both rough- and smooth-textured bark; it is positioned close to the top of the crotch, making sure there is enough thickness at the top to accommodate the shape. The shape of the crotch produces a particularly dramatic natural-edge bowl.

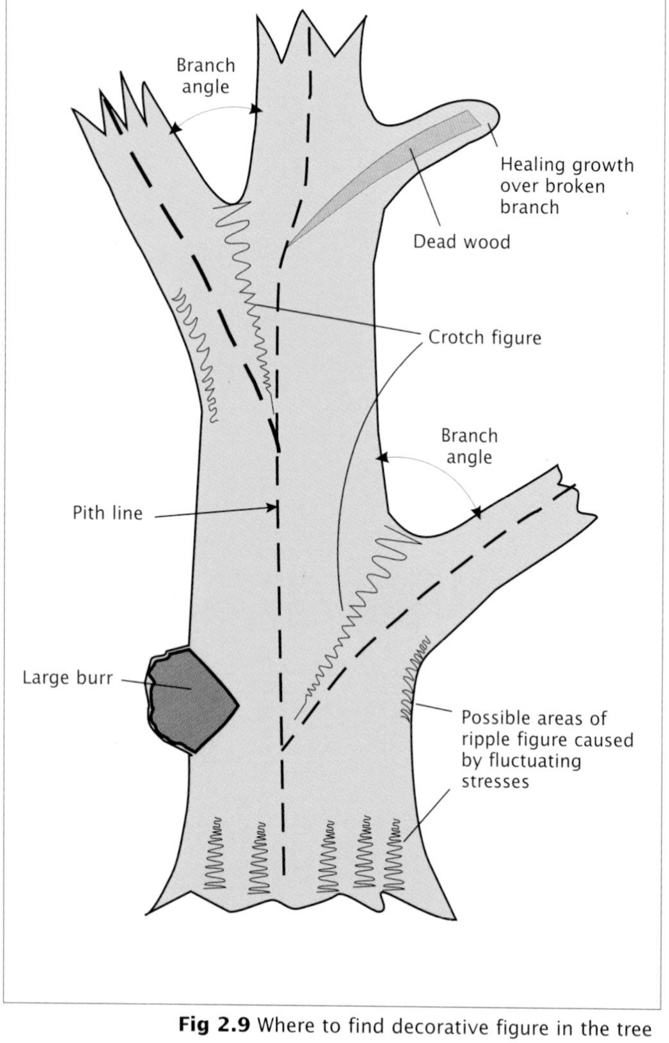

Ripple

Ripple occurs in the whole of some individual trees of species such as ash and sycamore. Ripple sycamore is sought-after by violin makers for making the backs of fiddles, which is why the ripple figure has become known as 'fiddle-back'.

In an average tree, ripple is sometimes found where there is movement close to a solid area, such as the bottom of the main trunk close to the ground, or where a branch leaves the main trunk (Fig 2.9). This is brought about by the tree's reaction to movement: the swaying of the tree or branch in the wind produces wavy, spring-like grain which is flexible.

Burrs

'Burr' is an English word for a type of growth on the side of the tree which is full of bud eyes. This type of growth is the tree's reaction to insect irritation under the bark; it is irregular compared with the normal tree growth, but regular within

Fig 2.9 Where to find decorative figure in the tree

Labels in figure:
Branch angle
Healing growth over broken branch
Dead wood
Crotch figure
Branch angle
Pith line
Large burr
Possible areas of ripple figure caused by fluctuating stresses

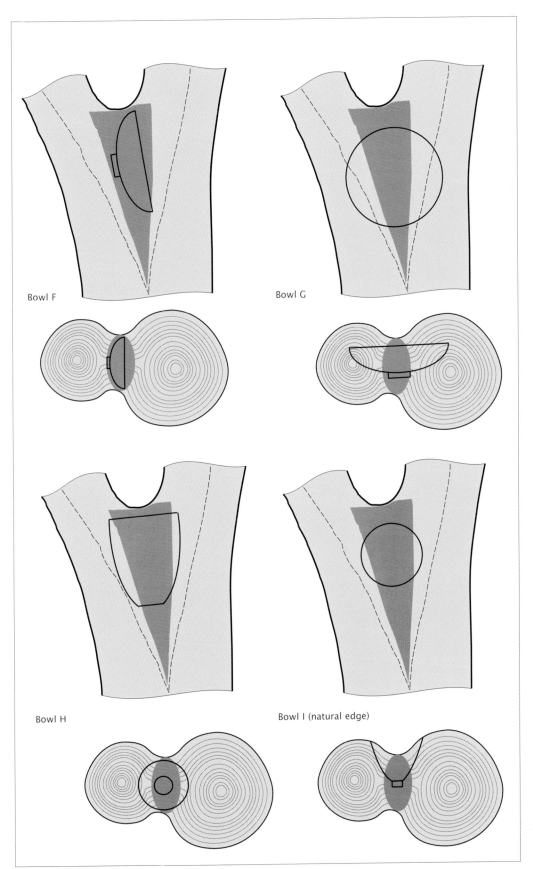

Bowl F

Bowl G

Bowl H

Bowl I (natural edge)

Fig 2.10 Different bowl orientations making use of crotch figure

Fig 2.11 Large burrs on the trunk of an elm tree

Fig 2.13 Bowls in the burrs: two possible orientations

Fig 2.12 An elm burr with the bark removed

itself (Figs 2.11 and 2.12). The burr appears as a large bulge on the side of the tree, but it also extends into the tree where it has been enclosed as the tree grows. As there is no particular grain orientation, bowls can be found anywhere within the burr. The irregular surface can make wonderful natural-edge rims. If the burrs are big enough they can be harvested from a standing tree by cutting them off close to the main trunk (Fig 2.13), taking care to avoid damaging the bark.

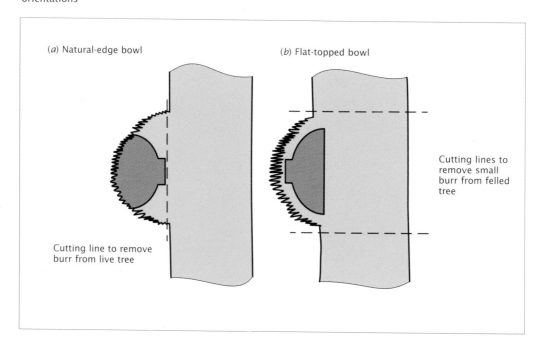

(*a*) Natural-edge bowl

(*b*) Flat-topped bowl

Cutting lines to remove small burr from felled tree

Cutting line to remove burr from live tree

Fig 2.14 Sycamore tree, showing healing growth over a broken branch

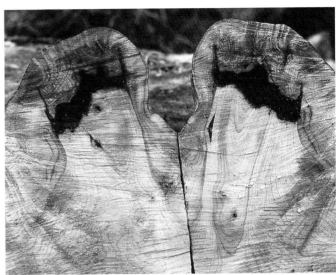

Fig 2.15 Inside view of a similar piece of healing growth

Burls

'Burl' is an American term referring to any type of growth on the side of a tree, *including* burrs. The term also includes healing growth over surface damage or broken and dead branches (Figs 2.14–2.16; see also Fig 2.9 on page 16). The latter can be used by holding the outside while turning out the dead insides, or the outside can be turned as well, to reveal the interesting grain pattern. In many cases it is a matter of examining the burl, then making an educated guess as to what is inside and proceeding on that basis.

Fig 2.16 A cross-grain natural-edge bowl in tulipwood, using healing growth as a feature

Spalting

'Spalting' describes the decorative pattern created in some woods by fungi as they decay (Fig 2.17). These effects are striking in plain woods where there is little or no difference in colour between sapwood and heartwood, such as beech, which produces magnificent spalting in an intricate pattern of fine black lines. This is greatly sought-after and can be more expensive than kiln-dried exotic wood when bought from a timber store. Sycamore and maple produce softer

Fig 2.17 Cross-grain dove bowl in spalted beech

spalting patterns, but holly is spectacular in its range of colours, from a soft orange through to deep purple in patches.

You might be lucky enough to find a spalted log which you can take home and turn; alternatively, there are two ways you can encourage spalting in fresh timber. The first is to store fresh logs in damp and preferably warm conditions for a few months, then investigate to see how they are getting on. The other method is to part-turn some bowls from fresh logs, then store them in damp wood shavings over a period of three to six months. As the bowls are being kept wet they will not shrink or distort, so the outside can be close to the finished size. If the centre of the bowl is left solid, then you can have a bowl with spalting on the outside and fresh wood on the inside. Bowls stored in this way often come out with a high moisture content – even higher than when you started – and they turn easily.

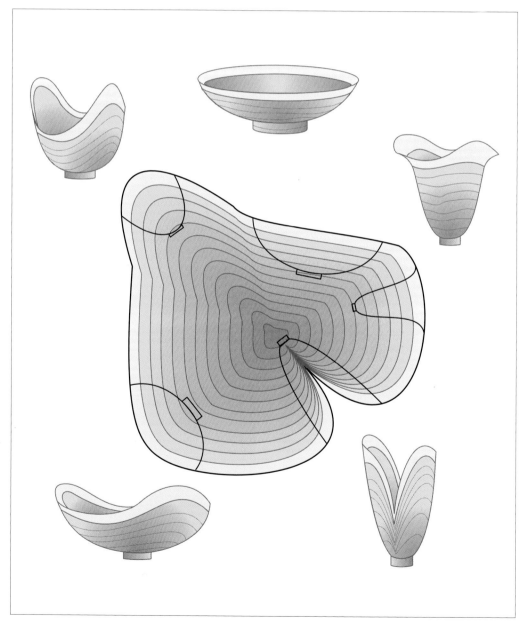

Fig 2.18 A log of irregular section offers many different possibilities for natural-edge cross-grain bowls

I have a short log of holly about 9in diameter by 12in long (230 x 305mm) which I have stored in a plastic bag (with holes in) with wet wood shavings. The end grain has become a rich jet black. I am now waiting for the inspiration to make a bowl from it.

By experimenting in these ways you can create your own exotic woods from plain, cheap timber, and it is fun. I call it 'controlled decay'.

The natural edge

On natural-edge bowls, the rim is the natural surface of the tree, usually including the bark and anything else on the surface, such as lichens. This type of bowl is exciting to turn, as it makes use of the whole tree from the outer surface right through to the heartwood. Combining all these aspects of the tree in one bowl gives it great depth, whether it be an end-grain or cross-grain bowl. The shape of the rim – which is the most important feature of the bowl – depends on the shape of the log selected, and how we position the bowl within the log.

Cross-grain bowls

Round trees make regular-shaped natural-edge bowls, and are a good starting point as they are easy to deal with. But many trees are not round, and while these do lead to further complications, they also present opportunities for an infinite variety of edge shapes and bowl designs. You can usually find a spot to make a flat-rimmed natural-edge bowl, or you can go to extremes to get maximum variations in the height of the rim.

Fig 2.18 shows an irregular log and the different natural-edge bowls that can be found in it, depending on which section of the tree they come from. These bowls can be discovered very easily with a piece of chalk and a little imagination. Draw a simple curved shape between any two points on the bark and a bowl will jump out at you. To explore the possibilities of natural-edge cross-grain bowls, all you need is a piece of chalk and some imagination.

To be a little more precise about the details of a natural-edge bowl: first decide what the maximum diameter of the bowl is to be – that is, the width measured across the *highest* parts of the rim. Mark this width across the log between points X and Y, then join them with the dotted datum line A (Fig 2.19a). (For simplicity's sake Fig 2.19 assumes that a round log is being used.) Next mark the centre of datum line A and draw a line B perpendicular to it, which is the centre line of the bowl. From the top end of line B – which is where the highest part of the rim will be on the finished bowl – measure down the centre line the required height of the bowl and draw in the base line parallel to the datum line A. Draw vertical lines from X and Y down to the base line: the area within these lines contains the bowl. You can now draw half the profile of the bowl (line D) from the top of the centre line to the bottom of one of the side lines. Line D represents half the front outline view of the bowl, showing the maximum diameter and maximum height. Retracing this same shape to the left of line B gives us line E, which represents half the side outline view. The place where line E meets the edge of the log marks the position of the rim's lowest point, and a second dotted datum line, C, can then be drawn across from here to represent the bowl diameter at that point. Continue line E across to the other side of the log to complete the bowl shape.

As the rim diameters are different at the highest and lowest points, the bowl will be oval, as shown in the top view (Fig 2.19b). The distance down the centre line from the top edge of the bark to the horizontal datum line C is a measure of the rim's rise and fall around the bowl. This distance is also a measure of the degree of difficulty in turning the bowl: the greater it is, the more difficult. As this bowl is from a round log, the rim rises and falls in a smooth curve.

We know from Fig 2.4 (bowl A) that the grain pattern will consist of concentric oval rings and that there will be three strata, from the bark, through the sapwood to the heartwood, which is an oval patch in the bottom (Fig 2.19*b* and *c*). In this way the bowl is on view before the chainsaw has touched the wood, and if you change your mind the chalk lines on the end of the log can be removed – so

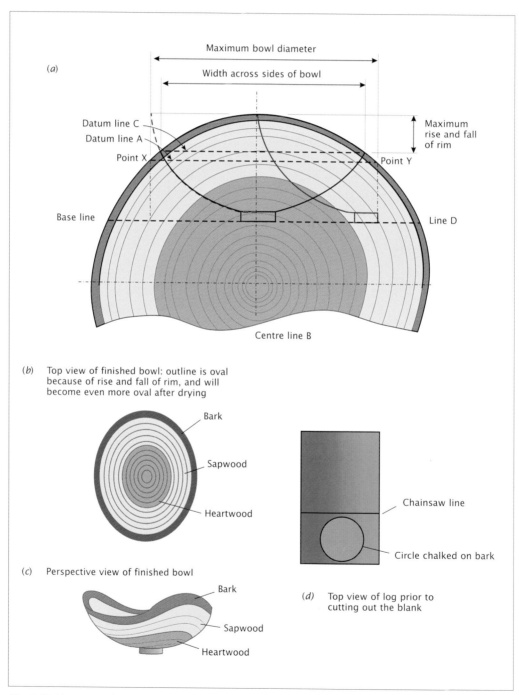

Fig 2.19 How to mark out cross-grain natural-edge bowls

you can try all the permutations there are without having to make them. Draw the circle in the bark (Fig 2.19d) only when you are committed to the bowl, as drawing this circle destroys other bowls.

Drawing the circle on the bark first is an alternative approach which you can use with experience, and is an appropriate procedure when you want to include particular surface features – such as depressions, small burrs or lichen – on the rim. The way to do this is to make sure that the circle goes through them. When you draw the circle with dividers, the shape which appears on the surface of the log won't be round, but it will be similar in shape to the turned rim, which won't be round either (unless the bowl is to have vertical sides). Having drawn the circle, project the edge lines to the end of the log, draw the datum lines and proceed as before.

End-grain bowls

Natural-edge end-grain bowls use the whole log section, which becomes the diameter of the bowl. While working this way round limits the size of tree that can be used to the diameter of the required bowl, it also means that small branches can be utilized. The shape of the natural edge is controlled by (a) the selection of the log and (b) the design of the bowl.

A round branch turned on centre produces a round, flat-topped natural-edge bowl, no matter what the rim angle. An oval-shaped branch also produces a flat-topped natural-edge bowl, if the rim angle is at 90° to the axis until it reaches solid wood. On the other hand, an oval-shaped branch produces a flowing edge with a rise and fall, and with its peaks at the widest points, provided the rim angle is less than 90° to the axis. Some of the possibilities are shown in Fig 2.20. The amount of rise and fall is controlled by the angle of the rim. A 90° rim gives a flat edge; as the rim angle becomes steeper, the rise and fall of the edge increases and

becomes more dramatic. One thing you need to keep in mind is that the steeper the entry angle, the taller the fragile bark edge becomes.

A triangular shape of branch produces three peaks (Fig 2.21). The more irregular the branch shape, the more interesting the edge. The inclusion of small branches is possible, or even the use of crotches – in which case each branch becomes a projecting 'wing'.

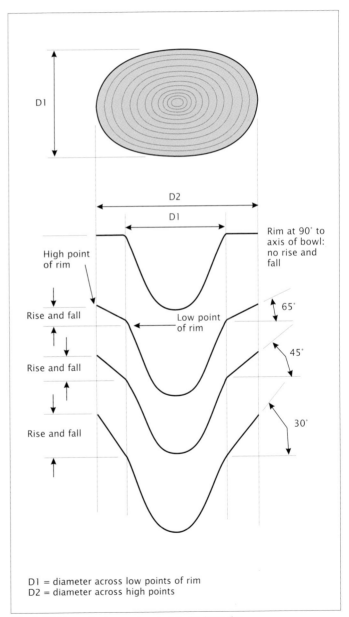

D1 = diameter across low points of rim
D2 = diameter across high points

Fig 2.20 Natural-edge end-grain bowls: how the angle of the rim determines the amount of rise and fall

Fig 2.21 Natural-edge end-grain bowl made from a branch of triangular section: this gives a rim with three peaks

Shrinkage, stress and distortion of bowls

As wood loses moisture it shrinks, on average, 0.1% longitudinally, 4% radially and 8% circumferentially (as we saw in Chapter 1). At the same time, internal stresses are introduced. These different shrinkage rates cause distortions in the drying timber, and therefore distortion is inevitable when bowls are turned green and then dried. The extent of shrinkage and distortion depends on the shape of the bowl and how it is positioned and orientated in the tree. If we take another look at bowls A, B, C, D and E (from Figs 2.2 and 2.3), with an even thickness of ¼in (6mm), we can see what happens to the bowls as they dry slowly and evenly.

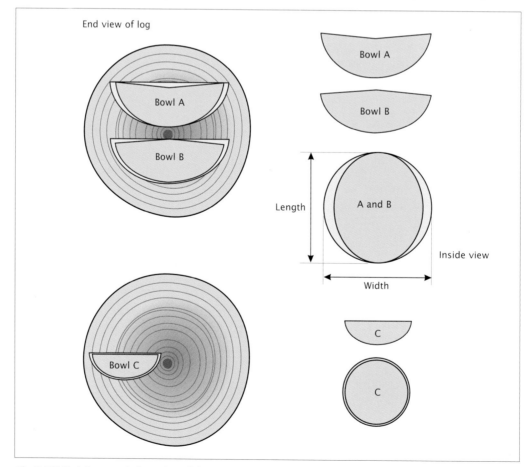

Fig 2.22 Shrinkage and distortion of the cross-grain bowls shown in Fig 2.2

Fig 2.23 Distortion caused by inclusion of juvenile wood. As the shrinkage of juvenile wood is less than that of the surrounding heartwood, it is likely to cause a bulge on drying

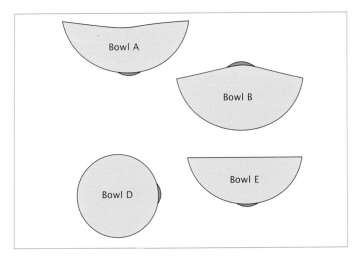

Cross-grain bowls

For bowl A, with its base next to the pith, the longitudinal shrinkage, which is minimal, can be ignored, so the length of the bowl remains the same (Fig 2.22). (Length is measured *along* the grain.) The radial shrinkage reduces the height and width of the bowl. (Width is measured *across* the grain.) The circumferential shrinkage causes the bowl to cup away from the pith, raising the height of the edge at either side and reducing the width. The juvenile wood may cause a slight bump in the bottom of the bowl (Fig 2.23). The final result is an oval bowl with the side edges cupped slightly upwards.

For bowl B, with the rim just below the pith, again, longitudinal shrinkage is minimal. Radial shrinkage reduces both the height and the width of the bowl. Circumferential shrinkage bends the rim away from the pith, lowering the edges at either side; this also reduces the diameter slightly. Distortion is considerable, as the radial shrinkage combines with the circumferential shrinkage to reduce the width, whereas the length of the bowl remains unchanged. The result is that the bowl is oval in plan, with a reduced height. The sides are lower than the ends; on top of this, the juvenile wood – which

shrinks less than the heartwood – creates a rounded peak at the pith point.

Both bowls A and B were placed symmetrically about the pith, giving mirror-image grain patterns and matching distortion on each side of the bowl, with the result that even though they will both distort they will still be symmetrical about the centre. Moving the bowls off-centre from the pith results in distorted, asymmetrical bowls.

Bowl C is placed in a situation where the shrinkages do not interact. The longitudinal shrinkage (which we ignore) takes place along the length of the bowl, the radial shrinkage reduces the width and the circumferential shrinkage reduces the height. The bowl will be oval, but less so than bowls A or B, and the rim remains flat.

End-grain bowls

The height of an end-grain bowl shrinks by an amount equal to the longitudinal shrinkage of the cells; this is negligible and can be ignored, irrespective of where in the log the bowl comes from.

In bowl D, the effect of both radial and circumferential shrinkage is to reduce the width and length by their respective amounts at 90° to each other (Fig 2.24).

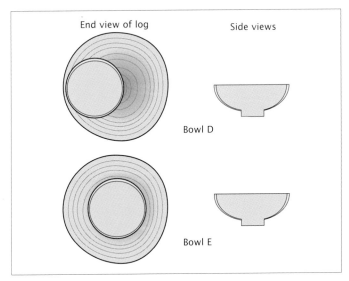

Fig 2.24 Shrinkage and distortion of the end-grain bowls shown in Fig 2.3

This should theoretically result in a slightly oval bowl, but in practice the ovalness at the rim is very slight.

In bowl E, with the pith in the middle, the radial and some of the circumferential shrinkage work together to reduce the rim diameter; the excess circumferential shrinkage reduces the rim diameter a little more, because the bowl centre is hollow, but it will still be round. In the solid base, the excess circumferential shrinkage creates internal stresses. The juvenile wood shrinks less than the heartwood, and this may cause a bulge in that area.

The average distortion of an end-grain bowl is less than for the equivalent cross-grain bowl. My wife and I found this to be of benefit, with the result that our present 'Coloured Series' of bowls are all end-grain.

Special distortions

All the above accounts of shrinkage and distortion are based on the assumption that the bowl thickness is great enough to be representative of the whole tree, so that the shrinkage of the bowl corresponds to the average shrinkage of the tree. But we know that different parts of the tree can have different shrinkage rates. Sapwood shrinkage may be greater than heartwood shrinkage, particularly when there is a difference in colour. The visual effect on a bowl is minimal where there is a horizontal split between heart and sapwood, but when the split is vertical – in either cross-grain or end-grain bowls – the bowls can become lopsided. The bark shrinkage is greater than that of the sapwood.

When the bowl is thin – say, less than ⅛in (3mm) – individual grain cells are no longer restrained in their shrinkage and movement by other cells around them, so they can move freely; this causes more irregular distortion, but at the same time minimizes internal stress. This is more obvious in 'weak' shapes, such as flat rims,

than in strong shapes such as spheres. Bowls with irregular grain patterns, such as are found in crotch wood, ripple grain and burr, show significant distortion because their grain orientation is constantly changing.

The drying process

All the shrinkage described above will happen as you dry a bowl from the fibre saturation point to the equilibrium moisture content; but the drying process needs to be considered carefully, as differential drying within the bowl can cause large internal stresses, with inevitable splitting. If a thick bowl is dried quickly, the outside dries first and shrinks, while the inside is still wet and remains the same size; the result is internal stresses and surface cracking. Or thin parts dry more quickly than thick parts, with similar results.

Controlling the drying process allows the moisture content to be reduced from above the fibre saturation point to a stable state at EMC in a safe manner. 'Stability' in this context means being at the EMC of the bowl's final environment, probably in the home. 'Safe' means maintaining a reasonably consistent moisture content throughout the bowl to avoid internal stresses.

Fig 2.25 shows the drying process carried out in one continuous operation. The red line shows the average moisture content for a drying bowl, and looks quite innocuous by itself. But if we look at the differential drying rate between the surface and the centre of that bowl, we see a very different picture. The difference in moisture content between inside and surface is considerable and would certainly cause internal stress and surface cracking. The thicker the bowl, the greater the difference.

A thin bowl with an even thickness of 1/16in (1.5mm) can be dried in 24 hours or even less without problems. I often do this by taking the thin bowls into the kitchen

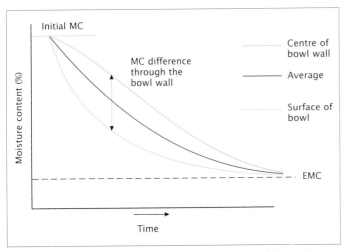

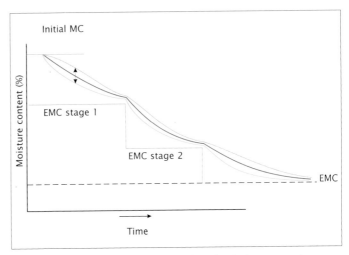

Fig 2.25 How uncontrolled drying leads to differential drying in different parts of the bowl

Fig 2.26 Using controlled drying to slow the drying rate and minimize differential drying

and putting them over the oil-fired Aga cooker (which is on all the time), where they dry very quickly. During the drying they can be heard crackling, but this causes little damage. A bowl which has been dried when it is very thin will have few internal stresses, as each part is able to shrink and move as it wishes. From experience of trying to break dry, thin, green-turned bowls, they are very much stronger than if they had been turned from a solid piece of dry wood.

Fig 2.27 Using the microwave to dry a part-turned bowl. Check the weight after each session

A bowl ¼in (6mm) thick needs to be dried more slowly, taking about a week to reach EMC.

Differential drying can be reduced by drying in stages with only a slightly lower EMC each time. For example, putting the bowl in a bag (paper rather than polythene) with wet wood shavings will lengthen the drying time, but also greatly reduce the differential drying. The piece should be monitored at regular intervals by weighing; when the weight is found to be stabilizing, the moisture content is also stabilizing and the piece can be moved to a second intermediate stage until the moisture content stabilizes again. Finally bring it into room conditions, again allowing it to stabilize before applying a finish or beginning the final turning (Fig 2.26).

A little more care should be taken with thicker bowls and with part-turned bowls, which could be up to 1½in (38mm) thick; I would slow the drying down further for these, allowing up to three months. Taking differences between species into account, I would dry holly and fruitwoods more slowly than sycamore, beech or ash.

Microwave drying

If you find air-drying a little slow, why not try microwave drying (Fig 2.27)? Thin bowls can be dried in a couple of minutes, which is a great advantage if you want instant results. To my mind, the great advantage of microwave drying for thin bowls is that they are very soft and pliable on being taken out of the oven, and can be moulded to the desired shape while the wood cools.

Drying in the microwave is not foolproof, so it is a good idea to follow a procedure and build up experience with the types of wood you use and the sizes of bowl you make. Weigh the bowl first. As a starting point for a part-turned bowl about 6in (152mm) diameter by 1½in (38mm) thick, put it in the microwave on medium power for about two minutes. On taking it out you will find it is warm, so put it in a cool place to cool down – the cooler the better – then weigh it again. Repeat the process until dry – but not too dry, as repeated microwave drying will bring the bowl down to 0% moisture content and may cause internal damage. Check your drying graph (recording time in the microwave) and stop before it levels out. Altogether this procedure could take 24 hours, as the cooling time could be long.

Relieving stresses

Stress is something that comes into the wood during the drying process and can eventually be destructive, causing distortion or cracking. These stresses can be relieved by steaming (as in steam bending), then allowing the wood to cool slowly. Stress-relieving is not necessary for most situations, but I would recommend it when making large, flat platters which are part-turned, as a flat rim is a very weak shape and much more liable to distortion than, say, a spherical shape. Stress-relieving on part-turned work should be done after the initial drying and before final turning. I would imagine that microwave drying also relieves the stresses within the wood.

Polyethylene glycol (PEG)

There is another method available for stabilizing the wood, which is different from seasoning in that the moisture in the wood is displaced by a solution known as polyethylene glycol (PEG). It is said to be suitable for part-turned bowls, which are submerged in the solution for up to three weeks, during which time the moisture in the timber is replaced through osmosis by the waxy substance of PEG. After soaking, the bowl is allowed to dry and is then ready for re-turning and finishing.

PEG was developed for stabilizing timbers from underwater archaeological wrecks when they are taken out of the water to be put on display to the public. It is essential to use PEG, or a similar solution, in a situation like this, as if they were left to dry naturally the timbers would crumble away.

Unfortunately, PEG is hygroscopic, and changes its viscosity with changes in temperature and humidity; consequently it will ooze out of the wood. In order to prevent this, the wood has to be completely sealed with a very hard finish such as polyurethane, which is very difficult to achieve because parts of the surface will not accept a finish. Even without this problem, the finishing restrictions alone make PEG unsuitable for many turned products, as a hard finish often detracts from the natural sheen and the tactile qualities of wood which we are hoping to achieve. In any case, I would prefer not to get such a substance on my hands or use it anywhere near food. The process takes just as long as natural drying of the part-turned bowl, and it does not solve any problems associated with natural drying without introducing greater problems or restrictions. It certainly costs a lot more in terms of the raw material, storage drums and handling – which in the end can be a lot more expensive than the piece of wood you are trying to preserve.

The solution to drying and stabilizing timber, whether turned in one operation or part-turned, lies in understanding the material and treating it sympathetically – not in your pocket!

3 Timber, tools and techniques

Sourcing and selecting timbers

The principal requirements in selecting the type of timber for green turning are no different from those for working dry: Is it suitable for the purpose of the final product? And is the price right? Whether wood is worked dry or green, the final product will be dry, so the same criteria apply. For example, if a bowl is to come into direct contact with food then the wood should be non-toxic, odourless, close-grained so as not to take food particles into the grain, and washable. Whether it is to be turned green or dry is irrelevant.

Other considerations, such as ease of machining or turning, are relevant in timber selection. In general, any timber that can be turned successfully dry will turn more easily green. Most timbers can be turned green, but some will be easier to work than others. I remember exchanging some sycamore for some apple from a neighbour's fuel pile and doubling my production rate because the apple worked so easily.

Hardwoods are used most for bowl turning, not just because they have the physical and decorative characteristics required by the turner, but because there is a greater choice of species, larger sizes can be obtained, and they are easily available. Timbers we might think of as shrubs or associate with hedgerows, such

as laburnum or hawthorn, are hardwoods and produce decorative turning timber. Fruitwoods turn especially well: apple, pear, cherry and plum might come to mind, but don't forget the guavas, mangoes, kiwi fruit and others – in fact, any kind of fruitwood is well worth trying.

But softwoods should not be neglected, as there are some spectacular ones used by turners and I am sure there are more waiting to be discovered. Yew turns beautifully when green. Its creamy-coloured narrow band of sapwood is in vivid contrast to the rich red of the heartwood. It also has an irregular-shaped trunk from which interesting natural-edge bowls can be made. Huon pine is one of the slowest-growing trees in the world and turns well; with its tight growth rings and rich, creamy, evenly coloured wood, it has its own beauty. The redwoods of Oregon and California are majestic in nature and produce fine turning timber, particularly from their burrs.

As the timber used for green turning comes in log form, and is therefore awkward to handle, heavy and in limited demand, it is unlikely that you can get supplies from your local timber merchant. Sawmills which handle fresh timber might help if you want large quantities or are willing to use slabbed timber, or there might be a specialist supplier within reasonable travelling distance who meets your needs. The most likely supplies of trees suitable for green turning are close at hand: in gardens, parks, on building sites, or anywhere that trees are grown for their natural beauty rather than their commercial value. Felling, pruning, house building, garden redesign, are going on all the time – talk to park keepers, council workers, tree surgeons, builders, and let them know that you are interested in fresh wood. They are usually helpful, especially if you cross their palm with silver or maybe a bowl or two. Try everything you can get your hands on to increase your experience and develop expertise. Contact with other woodturners gives you the opportunity to swap samples and widen your experience.

I think it is a good idea to use native timbers wherever you live, as it gives your work a national identity. The search for the exotic is usually a search for what is someone else's native timber. For our own work, we use timber from the Highlands of Scotland and Caithness, in particular that which has been felled for non-commercial purposes: wind-blown trees, trees cut down to make room for housing, prunings made to keep trees in control, are the sources of our timber. Even in a county with few trees I have found an adequate supply, mainly of sycamore, over the last 20 years.

Because of our philosophy, most of the timber available to us is sycamore, so our style of turning and decorating bowls has evolved from this. Guides to the properties of different timbers are listed in the Select Bibliography on page 129; the information given in these sources can be matched to the requirements of your products.

Harvesting green wood

'When is the best time to cut down a tree for green turning?' is a question I am asked regularly. It is one that I had never even answered for myself, because the question implies the luxury of having trees available to cut down at my leisure – a situation I have never been in. My answer to the question is usually 'When it's cheapest' or 'When it's available.' The last trees I bought were cut down in September, but that was not by choice. One Saturday morning I was driving back home through Castletown, a village five miles from where I live, and went past a new building site where they were just cutting down five sycamores to make room for one house. I immediately reversed up the road and back into the site, and after haggling for half an hour with the owner I bought all five. I was disappointed at having to pay for them, as I was hoping he would be pleased that I was prepared to move them from the site for him without charging. With the help of the site machinery and a tractor and trailer I took home approximately 25 tonnes of wood. This sequence of events is typical of how I get my wood supply (Fig 3.1).

But the question also deserves a more considered reply. The time of year when the tree is cut down does make a difference to some of its properties and to how it can be used. For green turners, bark retention is critical if one is going to make natural-edge bowls or vessels with the bark on. During the growing season the inner bark layer is active in transporting the tree's nutrients and the cambium layer is active

Fig 3.1 Harvesting sycamore from a building site at Castletown, Caithness

in producing new wood on one side and bark on the other. This is the time when the cambium layer is at its weakest, and obviously a time to avoid felling trees if you are looking for bark retention. During the winter, which is the dormant season, the cambium layer is stronger, which makes trees felled at this time suitable for uses where bark retention is desirable.

If you are looking for ease of cutting, then my preference is to use active, summer-felled wood – though there is no scientific evidence to support this idea. Moisture content does not change much through the year, but the higher it is, the easier the cutting. The timber will also remain wet for longer when stored.

> **Felling trees is a tricky and dangerous operation; I would not advise you to undertake it unless you are trained in the safe use of chainsaws for tree felling and clearing. You will also need to have all of the protective clothing: steel-toecapped boots, special trousers and jacket made from fibres which will clog up the chainsaw if it touches them, gloves, and a helmet with visor and earmuffs. Buy them at the same time as you buy the chainsaw, as accidents will not wait to happen until you have them. If you are going to fell trees near property, then insurance is essential – and it may be difficult to get.**

You can manage with a bush saw (a tubular steel bow saw) if you are only using small lumber and the logs are light enough to be physically picked up and cut with a deep-throated bandsaw. But it won't be long before you realize that a chainsaw, properly and carefully used, is an essential green woodturning tool, as it enables you to harvest, collect and prepare the wood for the lathe.

A phone call to say that a tree is being cut down or cleared, and would you like

Fig 3.2 An elm tree with burr, spoiled by the inclusion of fence wire

it, is invariably a very tempting offer, but it is advisable to evaluate the tree first. Is it of a size and species that will be useful when you get it home? View the tree before deciding, as there are a number of potential problems which, at best, could cause a lot of frustration, expense and time-wasting. Trees growing in gardens have often been used for swings, washing lines, target practice and tree houses, and are quite likely to have a large number of foreign bodies such as 6in nails embedded in them. Many of these will be covered by an inch or two of growth, and well beyond detection by the eye or hand – although a metal detector may pick them out. It is easy to see that the blade of a chainsaw can be badly damaged if it catches any of these. A lumberyard is most unlikely to slab garden-grown timber for you, as the potential for damage, particularly to the saw blade, is far in excess of the value of the tree. This also applies to trees around the perimeter of fields or paddocks, as they are often used for posts and strainers, and many yards of fencing material can be embedded in them (Fig 3.2).

Having evaluated the tree, it is a good idea to look at the access. Can you get your truck and trailer alongside the tree, and is there any machinery available to lift the logs? Situations to avoid are where the timber has to be cut into small pieces so that it can be thrown over a high fence, or even carried through the house, to reach the transport.

Once the tree is lying on the ground it is then a question of cutting it up, transporting it home and storing it ready for use. An essential priority when cutting up the tree is always to leave the logs as big and as long as you can possibly handle and store. You are always going to lose an inch or two off the ends of the log after it has been stored for a while, and losing 2in (50mm) off each end of a 12in (305mm) long log severely limits what you can do with it, whereas losing 2in off the ends of a 10ft (3m) log is neither here nor there.

Look carefully around the tree and select the sections of timber that you want to preserve, then with a piece of chalk mark the points where you are going to cut, to be sure of getting the best out of the tree for your particular products. It might seem easy enough to start by cutting off all the branches close to the trunk, but don't: you will render most of the crotch figure unusable. Cut large branches off as shown in Fig 3.3, as this will allow you to make full use of the crotch wood. Doing it this way certainly makes moving the log much more difficult, but you will reap the rewards in your finished pieces. Mark up the cutting points clearly, so you will not have to think about them once the chainsaw is running. Never leave this operation to anyone else, as they could ruin what might otherwise have been an excellent piece of timber.

If you are interested in making natural-edge bowls, then what you are seeing when you look at the logs is the finished rims of all the bowls you are going to make, so careful handling is very important. Don't use aggressive machinery or chains directly on the wood. Lift the log on planks if you are using a forklift or digger bucket. Use ropes rather than chains for lifting, but whichever you use, wrap plenty of sacking around the log first. Even if you are not making natural-edge bowls, it is still advisable to avoid damage to the bark, as this is a protective layer which will hold in the moisture and prevent rapid drying of the log surface; without it, the log is likely to split.

Storage

It's a great feeling to cut down a tree then turn it into finished products on the same day. As this is not always possible or even practical – and can only account for a small proportion of the tree anyway – the wood usually has to be stored until it

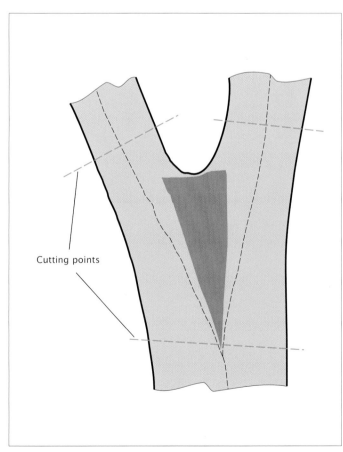

Fig 3.3 Where to cut the log to make best use of crotch figure

Cutting points

is wanted. In the green state the logs have a limited shelf life, which can either be extended or reduced depending on the method of storage chosen.

Methods of storage are very much dependent on your local environment and climate, and for short-term storage the time of year can be important. The logs should be stored 'in the round' – do not split them in half, as this will cause rapid drying and you will lose much of the flexibility in utilizing the timber. Protect it from the elements to reduce moisture loss, avoid direct sunlight, high temperature, low humidity, and drying winds. Storage undercover in a damp, shaded, cool location will provide ideal conditions. Where there is an earth floor, the logs are best raised above this, as excessive dampness on the outside of the bark will cause it to decay quickly and come loose. Painting the ends with something that will reduce moisture loss is a good idea: most kinds of paint, wax or oil can be used, and there is no need to buy expensive proprietary products which will probably cost you more than the lumber in the first place. Part-cans of paint left over from decorating the house or painting the car – which are useless but which you are loath to throw away – will do the job adequately, and you can sleep easy knowing that you have put the paint to some good use. Don't pile the logs on top of each other, as that is likely to cause damage, and usually the one that you want first will be right at the bottom of the pile. Standing them on end can be economical on space, and covering logs with damp sacks will improve the storage conditions if they are otherwise less than ideal. Now that the wood is nicely stored away, you can relax while you plan what you are going to do with it.

Turning the wood as soon as possible after felling is the best way to retain the natural colours and contrasts within the wood for your finished products. Once the tree is cut down it begins to die and

eventually decay. Most timbers will become completely useless after a time, but before they reach that stage some woods – particularly the less decorative ones such as beech, holly, sycamore, maple, etc. – can be greatly enhanced in appearance as the decay and fungal patterns creep into the wood. This can be encouraged by providing warm, damp conditions, but it is unlikely that you will be able to retain the bark as well as having the spalting.

Tools of the trade

Whatever you are planning to make on the lathe, there are always a number of different tools that can be used, different techniques and different holding methods that can be employed. Indeed, it is often assumed that every woodturner will use his own unique tools and technique, even though the finished products might be identical to those made by many other turners. But when you look closely at how woodturners work, the methods are not so different – it is just that some are doing it better than others. Each turner should look for the most effective and efficient methods of achieving a particular result, and the choice of tools and equipment plays a large part in that.

Turning tools

Although there is a bewildering array of tools for the woodturner, it is best to work with a few tools, but make sure that they are the right ones for the job. I have listed in Table 2 (page 36) the tools I would recommend for the green turning of bowls, together with the lengths of the handles. The shapes to which they should be sharpened are illustrated in Figs 3.4 and 3.5. Both bevel shape and handle length are important factors in making the tool right for the job.

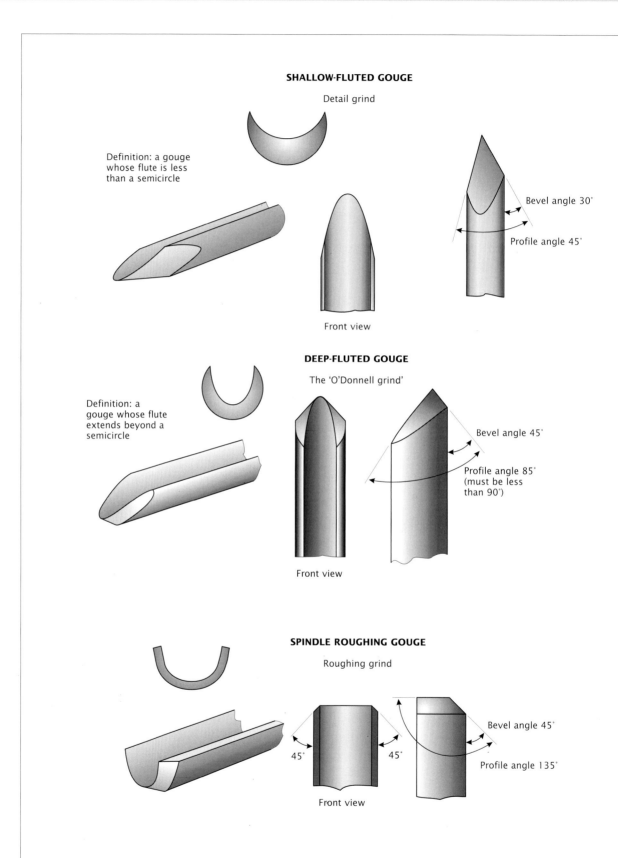

Fig 3.4 Recommended sharpening profiles for the seven basic tools

SCRAPERS

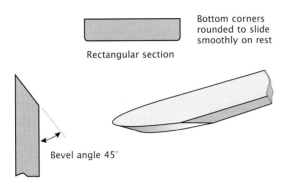

Rectangular section

Bottom corners rounded to slide smoothly on rest

Bevel angle 45°

| **SQUARE-ENDED SIDE-CUT, LEFT-HAND** | **ROUND-ENDED SIDE-CUT, LEFT-HAND** | **SKEW, LEFT-HAND** |

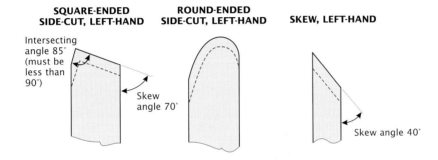

Intersecting angle 85° (must be less than 90°)

Skew angle 70°

Skew angle 40°

PARTING TOOL

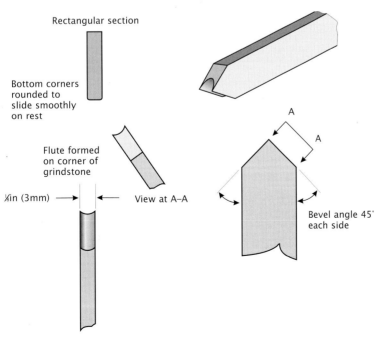

Rectangular section

Bottom corners rounded to slide smoothly on rest

Flute formed on corner of grindstone

⅛in (3mm)

View at A–A

A

A

Bevel angle 45° each side

Fig 3.5 A selection of tools suitable for green turning. *Left to right*: spindle roughing gouge, left-hand side-cut round-ended scraper, left-hand square-ended scraper, skew scraper, parting tool, shallow-fluted gouge, deep-fluted gouge

Table 2: Tools of the trade

Description	Size		Handle length	
	in	mm	in	mm
Deep-fluted gouge	½	13	18	457
Shallow-fluted gouge	½	13	14	356
Spindle roughing gouge	1¼	32	18	457
Parting tool	⅛	3	8	203
Scrapers				
Round-ended, side-cut, left-hand	1½	38	18	457
Square-ended, left-hand	1½	38	18	457
Skew, left-hand	1	25	14	356

Holding methods
(Figs 3.6 and 3.7)

I am a believer in the use of chucks, as they increase the range of work that can be tackled and they improve production rates. It is not just a matter of having a chuck, but of having a *chucking system*, which you can gradually build up over the years to cover all your requirements.

Multi-screw chucks
The foundation for any chucking system is the **multi-screw chuck** or **faceplate** (Fig 3.8). This went out of fashion in the early 1980s with the introduction of multi-function chucks, but it has seen a revival in the 1990s with the arrival of the power

Fig 3.6 Chucks suitable for green turning

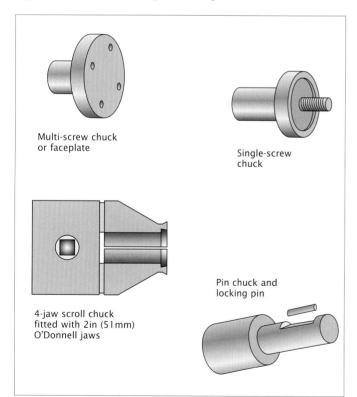

Multi-screw chuck or faceplate

Single-screw chuck

4-jaw scroll chuck fitted with 2in (51mm) O'Donnell jaws

Pin chuck and locking pin

Fig 3.7 Chucks suitable for green turning. *Left to right*: single-screw chuck, pin chuck (locking pin not shown), multi-screw chuck, 4-jaw scroll chuck with O'Donnell jaws

Fig 3.8 The basic multi-screw chuck, or faceplate

Fig 3.9 A single-screw chuck with parallel screw

screwdriver, which makes it an efficient holding method. For some turning situations the faceplate by itself is the best chucking method to use, providing the right size of plate and the right type of screws are used. A 4in (102mm) diameter multi-screw chuck will meet most requirements. Larger ones tend to be cumbersome and prevent access around the base of the bowl, although they are necessary for very large work.

Slotted screws are awkward to use with a power screwdriver, as it is easy for the driver to slip out. A Phillips-type driver or the Canadian Square driver are better; alternatively, use hexagon-headed screws, which give a positive drive using the socket on the screwdriver, then if necessary use a hand wrench just to check the final tension. For cross-grain and heavy end-grain work, a heavy, coarse-threaded screw, such as a coach bolt, is ideal. On light end-grain work, particularly with soft woods, I use a lighter and finer-threaded screw, as used for fibreboards, as these grip better in the end grain. The faceplate can also be used with waste blocks and glue, which is appropriate for some situations.

Single-screw chucks
These are an important class of chucks, which have great holding power and are particularly good for holding on the top of a bowl while turning the outside. The design is critical: about 3½in (89mm) diameter, with a rim and a good-size parallel screw. Once the chuck is on the lathe, turning blanks can be mounted and demounted quickly, providing you have first drilled the correct size of pilot hole. This is a simple, cheap and effective holding method. My preference is to have an independent single screw as shown in Fig 3.9.

Pin chucks
Pin chucks actually consist of two pins: a large centre one which provides strength and location, while the second pin locks into the bowl. There are two sizes available: 1in and 1½in (25 and 38mm). The 1in model with a flat pin recess is generally ineffective when turning green, as the locking pin tends to be so small that it buries itself into the soft green wood, allowing the wood to rotate on the large pin. The 1½in pins are effective, and I have used them to turn irregular-shaped blanks 20in in diameter by 6in tall (508 x 152mm) with complete security. If the piece is too small to be held on the 1½in pin chuck, then a 1in pin with two locking pins will work, or often a single-screw chuck can be used. Again I prefer an independent pin chuck

Fig 3.10 A substantial pin chuck, showing the recess for the locking pin on top

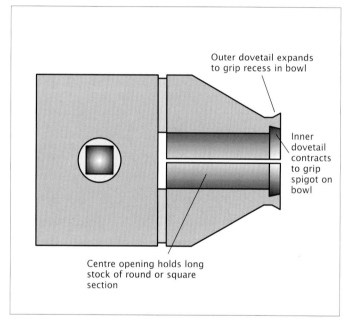

Outer dovetail expands to grip recess in bowl

Inner dovetail contracts to grip spigot on bowl

Centre opening holds long stock of round or square section

Fig 3.11 The principle of the 4-jaw scroll chuck with O'Donnell jaws

(Fig 3.10), which is better for turning heavy or natural-edge bowls.

Expanding and contracting chucks

These are two important methods of holding the wood. The expanding jaws grip in a dovetailed recess in the timber, while the contracting jaws grip onto a dovetailed spigot. The ease of use of either of these depends on the chuck design, which dictates the amount the jaws can move, the degree of accuracy to which the spigot or recess has to be made, and the ease of operation of the chuck, whether it works with levers or with a key. My preference is for a self-centring, four-jaw, key-operated scroll chuck, as these are easy to use and have considerable jaw movement. The compression jaws are the best for bowl turning, as they do not interfere with the design of the bowl (Figs 3.11 and 3.12).

Wooden jaw plates can also be used on the four-jaw scroll chuck, and are an ideal method for holding finished bowls on the rim while the base is refinished. Wooden segments are screwed onto the wood jaw plates, and dovetailed steps are turned in them to suit a range of bowl diameters. These can be designed to work either by expansion or contraction, depending on the shape of the rim (Figs 3.13–3.15). When turning these steps, the jaws of the scroll chuck should be at the midpoint of their travel, so that when the wooden jaws are in use they can either expand or contract from their nominal size. To achieve this, the metal plates should be gripped onto a cross-shaped former approximately ¼in (6mm) thick to hold them in position while the wooden jaws are turned (Fig 3.16).

Fig 3.12 A 4-jaw scroll chuck, with two of the O'Donnell jaws removed to show inside

Fig 3.13 Home-made wooden jaws for the 4-jaw scroll chuck, used for holding bowls by the rim whilst turning the base

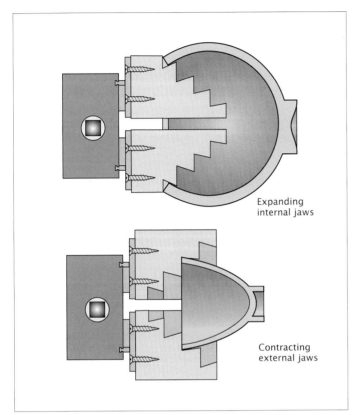

Expanding internal jaws

Contracting external jaws

Fig 3.15 External wooden jaws for use in the contracting mode, with two of the jaws removed to show inside

Fig 3.14 Internal wooden jaws for use in the expanding mode

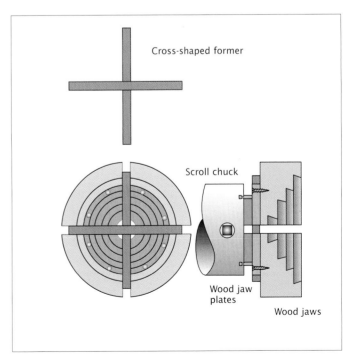

Cross-shaped former

Scroll chuck

Wood jaw plates

Wood jaws

Fig 3.16 Turning the wooden jaws; the metal plates are gripped onto a cross-shaped wooden former to ensure that they are at the midpoint of their travel

Other useful equipment

- Bush saw
- Power screwdriver with hex-head socket
- Hand-held electric drill, 3,000rpm, for power sanding
- 2 and 3in (51 and 76mm) soft power-sanding pads
- 3in (76mm) sanding discs, 100, 120, 180 and 240 grit. The 3in discs will fit on the 2in pad, and can be folded round the side for use on narrow and straight-sided work
- Movable lamp, for shining through the wood to gauge thickness
- Rigid white plastic sheeting, for mounting behind the work to aid visibility, especially when working on intermittent edges

An essential addition to my workshop equipment when I started turning green wood was a watering-can with which I keep the wood moist while turning, to prevent it drying and distorting on the lathe. An unheated workshop also helps to reduce the drying rates – but in winter I find it necessary to use warm water in the can.

> **I find the watering-can safe to use on my Graduate lathes, because all the electrics are enclosed in a cast-iron base. Never apply water to the work on a lathe where the electrics are exposed, or where water is likely to get to them.**

Finishing equipment

Most woodturning finishes have almost instant drying properties, and are applied while the work is still on the lathe; the revolving piece gives easy access to the whole surface, and great buffing power. But pieces which have already dried and changed in shape cannot be finished in the lathe, so finishes have to be applied

and buffed by hand, or by other means such as spraying. A small compressor and spray equipment makes it possible to use some of the quick-drying lacquers where a hard finish is required.

Techniques

The deep-fluted gouge

Probably 99% of the turning on the projects in this book is done with the ½in (13mm) deep-fluted gouge and the swept-back grind. To get the best out of this tool:

- Set the toolrest about ⅜in (10mm) below centre (though this is only critical when you are working close to the axis of the lathe) and about ½in (13mm) away from the wood.
- Put the tool horizontally on the rest with the bevel pointing in the direction of cut.
- Stand behind the tool, looking down the bevel, in a dynamic stance and ready to 'work away from yourself'.
- Make firm and positive cuts.

Sheer scraping

Scrapers are essential tools, but there are times when the surface they produce leaves something to be desired. The finish can be greatly improved by using the scraper in a **sheer** attitude (I use 'sheer' in the sense of 'steep').

In regular scraping the tool is laid flat on the rest with the top facing the rotating wood, giving a cutting angle of 90°. In sheer scraping the tool is twisted onto one edge at approximately 70° to the rest, with the angle between the face of the tool and the face of the wood about 60–80° – certainly less than 90°, otherwise there is a risk of a dig-in (Fig 3.17). Take up a dynamic stance with the hand or arm firmly on the rest for good control, then draw the tool lightly but firmly across the surface. Once having made contact, move the tool alternately backwards and forwards across the surface, as it will cut the same whichever way it is moving, and this will help to build a rhythm (Fig 3.18).

Tool sharpening

Turning green wood, which tends to be soft, requires the tools to be very sharp all the time. I sharpen my tools a little at regular intervals – every few minutes – on a high-speed grinder. This means having the grinder close to the lathe and set higher than the lathe. A calibrated toolrest speeds up sharpening, as it takes the guesswork out of the tool angles. Wheels are also important: ruby wheels are sharper than other wheels, cut cooler and faster, and are ideal for both high-speed steel and carbon tool steel. Use 80 grit for sharpening, 46 grit for reshaping tools.

Fig 3.17 Sheer scraping with the 1½in (38mm) right-hand skew scraper

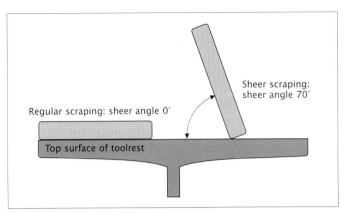

Sanding

I think it is a mistake to regard sanding as just a 'finishing' process, when it is actually the last wood-removal procedure in the turning process. Sandpaper should be considered as a valid turning tool in the same way as a gouge or chisel, and should be used in a similar way.

Fig 3.18 Sheer scraping in progress

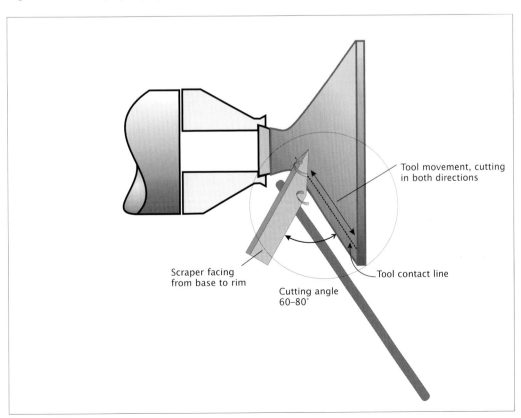

Pre-sanding check

Before starting the sanding process, the piece should be examined very closely to make sure that it is ready. Check any torn grain, and decide whether it can best be removed by the tool or by abrasives. Check the shape to make sure it is right, as sanding is a very poor shaping process. I hope that during the turning procedures you kept your hands clean, particularly when it came down to the finish cut; dirt from the hands is easily transferred to the wet wood, where it penetrates beneath the surface, making a permanent stain which really requires another cut to get rid of it. Only when you are satisfied that the piece is ready for sanding should you start – once sanding is under way there is no going back to using cutting tools, because very small pieces of abrasive do get into the wood and will very quickly blunt any tool put to it.

Wet sanding

Having turned the wood green, it will still be wet when you come to sanding – particularly if you have kept it moist with liberal applications of water. This gives the option of sanding 'wet' – a particularly attractive option, as it eliminates all the dust and the need for personal protection which are associated with dry sanding. It is a pleasurable process (with warm water, of course), and the wood will not dry and distort while you are working. Items such as the natural-edge goblet in Chapter 10 require sanding during the turning process, so wet-sanding is particularly appropriate.

There are abrasives which are especially suitable for wet sanding, usually cloth-backed (as used on belts for sanding machines), with a water-resistant resin glue. The kind I use for the heavy work is a 3M-ITE resin-cloth JWT aluminium oxide, which is a red-brown colour – the same colour as the power-sanding pads available.

Start with a coarser grit than you would on dry wood (80 grit instead of 100), and keep a bucket of water and a small, stiff brush by you for washing the abrasive regularly. Lightweight cloth should be used with the finer grits. When the wood is thin, always support it with the other hand to avoid bending and breaking the bowl. When you have finished, give the piece a good wash in clean water before drying.

Alternatively, there is a special abrasive for using wet or dry, which is known as 'wet-and-dry'. It is intended for use on metals and automotive paintwork, but can work very well on wood. The big disadvantage is that the abrasive is black, and small amounts coming off the paper will get into the grain of all but the hardest woods, where it will show up as tiny black specks in light-coloured woods. It could be used on dark and very close-grained woods.

Another option is to sand without the water, allowing the abrasive backing to absorb moisture so that the surface will dry. Again, the first step is best done with a coarser grit and heavier backing paper than you would use on dry wood (80 grit); work it until dust is generated, then work down through the grits: 100, 150 or 180, then 240. The problem with this method is that it can be expensive in abrasives to dry the surface, particularly if the wood is thick.

Dry sanding

A third option is to dry the surface using a hot-air gun intended for stripping paint, or even a hair dryer. The drying can be seen by a change in surface colour. Once dry, the surface can be sanded in the ordinary way.

Whichever process you choose to use, the method of applying the abrasive is similar. The rough grits are used to get rid of surface defects and tool marks; they are also used to smooth the surface and take out any ripples. Wrapping the abrasive around some dry shavings or a piece of cloth will help it to ride over the tops of the high spots and level them out. For finishing with the finer grits, the fingers should press directly onto the abrasive so that it follows the contours of the surface. I don't think there is any advantage in using grits finer than 240, as the finish requires a 'key' into the wood and the 240 will provide this.

Power sanding

Power sanding is ideal when the surface of the wood is dry, particularly on the larger, open-shaped bowls. It can be excellent for natural-edge bowls, as good drill control and light pressure give sharp edges all round. When sanding inside a bowl, put the toolrest across the front of the bowl and as far away from it as possible, then rest the forearm on the toolrest and hold the drill near the chuck. The other hand is the trigger hand. This stance will give you the good control which is necessary particularly for natural-edge bowls. When sanding the outside, tuck your elbows in close to your side and move the whole body to work the surface. You will need a drill running at around 3,000rpm, sanding pads of 2 and 3in (51 and 76mm) diameter, and sanding discs in a selection of grits from 80 to 240.

I have recently taken to power-sanding while the wood is still wet, but using air as a power source. **Never use an electric drill for wet power-sanding.**

Finishing

Most items will require some form of finish to protect the surface and bring out the natural beauty in the wood.

Having turned the piece green, parted it off and dried it, it is not possible to put it back in the lathe to apply the finish – not just because you will have cut off the mounting, but because the piece will no longer be round. By this time the surface will be dry, and you may find it necessary to give it a quick rub over with a fine sandpaper – a well-worn 240 or 400 grit – to give it a smooth feel.

The finishes available are just the same as for dry-turned wood – the only difference is that you will not be able to apply them on the lathe. And it will not be possible to apply very quick-drying lacquers by hand, as they will dry while you are applying them and thus leave lots of smears which will be very difficult to get rid of.

There are five basic options:

1 Don't put any finish on at all. This is fine for breadboards and rolling pins, but decorative pieces will soon get dirty and will be difficult, if not impossible, to clean.

2 Use an edible oil finish. This is ideal for items which will be in contact with food.

3 Use a non-edible oil finish such as Danish oil or tung oil. These seal the surface, bring out the colour and leave a nice soft feel to the surface. They may need reapplying from time to time.

4 Apply a wax over the oil finish. This gives a further protective coating with a nice sheen. The wax needs to be in a soft paste form, and to give the best surface it must be polished as soon as applied.

5 Hard finishes give the best protection to the piece and make later cleaning and maintenance very easy. These are best applied by spraying. The equipment need not be sophisticated, and you can get it for the price of a couple of large gouges. The real problem is where to spray. A spray booth with an extraction filter and a waterfall would be ideal, but prohibitive on cost. Spraying outdoors could be a solution, particularly if you are under cover and it is raining. Wherever you spray, always wear a good face mask.

We decorate most of our pieces with water-based dyes, then finish with three spray coats of Craftlac melamine. This is a cellulose lacquer with melamine particles to give it strength and hard-wearing properties.

4 Planning the work

The overall plan

The making of any bowl starts with an overall plan, which sets out the working path to be followed, at the end of which the bowl you expected will emerge. Each step of the plan takes into consideration all the subsequent steps, so that they can all be carried out without impeding the process at some later stage. The plan also takes into account the tools and equipment you have available, as well as your turning skills.

There are five stages to the plan:

1 Design
2 Planning the process
3 Sizing the blank
4 Material selection
5 Making the piece

If you follow this sequence each time, you will find the whole process enjoyable and rewarding.

1 Design

Don't be put off by the word 'design', with its connotations of doing accurate drawings and sketches requiring draughtsmanship skills. That's fine if you can do that, but all that is necessary are some rough dimensioned sketches (Fig 4.1). Using squared paper can help with scale and make things a lot easier. Then, if you don't like what you have drawn, a rubber (eraser) can easily change it. In this way, your design will develop into a resolved idea much more easily and with less frustration than when you are working with wood on the lathe. Once you are happy with the drawing, then you can proceed to make it on the lathe. Keeping the sketches is a good idea, just in case you have to repeat the piece; it is also a good starting point from which to develop ideas further.

The design stage is the most important step in the whole process of making a bowl: get this wrong and, no matter how good you are with the tools, the outcome will not be as good as it could be. Technique is a means to an end, and not the end in itself.

How many times have I heard something like this? 'I put a piece of wood in the lathe, then stand back and let it speak to me before I decide what to make from it. "A candlestick" or "a four-poster bed", "an egg cup" or "a salad bowl", I hear it shout.' Once the wood is in the lathe, all the major design decisions have been made – or, more likely, avoided. Specifying the timber is part of the design; orienting the grain is part of the design; size is part of the design. Preparing the wood for the lathe and selecting the appropriate holding methods are part of the manufacturing process to achieve a particular design. The design should have been completed long before the log was cut with the chainsaw, and that is when the wood should be speaking to you. Once the wood is in the lathe it is only possible to tinker with the design – and tinkering usually means that the design was not properly resolved in the first place.

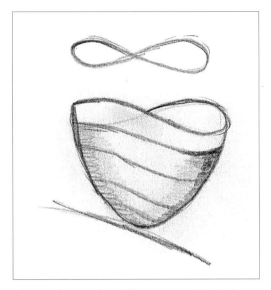

Fig 4.1 *(here and on following pages)* 'Design' need not be an intimidating process – rough pencil sketches like these are all that is needed

see an object is 'How was it made?', you have probably missed the beauty of the object. Just take in all you can, then let it flow out from you at some later stage. Imitation is a good way of learning, as it requires the disciplines of examination and understanding of form; but use it as a datum from which to develop your own recognizable style.

Starting points for design can vary, but it is very common to begin with a requirement for a functional object, such as a bowl to hold fruit or sugar. This is called a **design requirement**. Taking the fruit bowl as an example, ask yourself a few simple questions which will push the design along quickly:

How much fruit do we want it to hold?

This will depend on how many are in the family, and whether you are big fruit eaters, and it will determine what size of bowl you want.

Will it be holding a mixture of fruits, or just one type?

A bowl holding a mixture of fruits will need to be an open bowl, so that they are all visible. A bowl holding one type of fruit can be a more closed shape, so long as the fruit is easily accessible.

However, design does not start with a blank piece of paper. It starts with experience: experience of objects that you like or don't like, getting to know them and determining which elements are which within them. Everyday objects are important, as are visits to museums and art galleries. Don't just look at wood: glass, ceramics and metals offer a wealth of inspiration. Go round looking for things you like, and don't worry about how to make them. If the first question that comes to mind when you

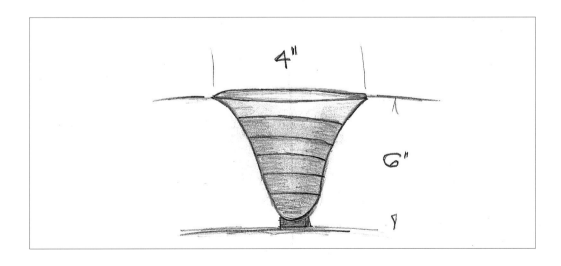

You can now consider the properties of wood suitable for this project, and match them to the timber you have available. Wood that is likely to come into direct contact with food should be tasteless and odourless, as well as washable. Colour and grain patterns in the wood should also be specified in order to match existing furniture. Gathering this information and writing it down will focus your mind on the situation in hand and help you develop your design ideas to a point where you can start to make sketches of the bowl shape. It is at this point that previous experiences should flow out through the pencil. And don't forget to specify the type of finish that will be most suitable.

For natural-edge bowls, and others for which the design requires special features of the timber, the log becomes an extension of the drawing paper as well as a source of inspiration. With a piece of chalk in hand, and experience flowing through the fingers, bowls can be revealed while they are still in the log.

There are some design considerations which apply particularly to green-turned objects, such as the effects of subsequent drying. Differential drying creates a lot of problems: outer surfaces dry quicker than the internal parts, thin parts dry quicker than thick parts; fine-edged rims on thick bowls are vulnerable, as they dry quickly; so are beads and other such fine details. This does not mean to say that you should avoid these features, but you should look for ways to limit the problem, such as controlling the drying process. This should be specified in section 2 of your master plan.

The design stage is a critical part of the process, so make it a positive one and it will become important in the development of your woodturning.

2 Planning the process

This part of your overall plan should contain all the operations necessary to make the bowl according to your design. Include everything from the first cuts with the chainsaw to applying the final finish, specifying the tools and chucking methods to be used. This sequence must be planned so as to take into account the tools and equipment available. The number of pieces required will affect whether the bowls are to be made individually or in batches. A typical sequence for a single bowl would be:

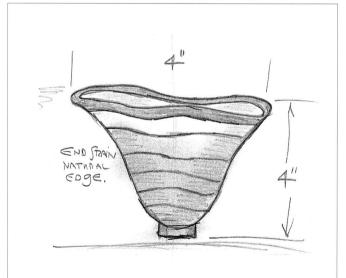

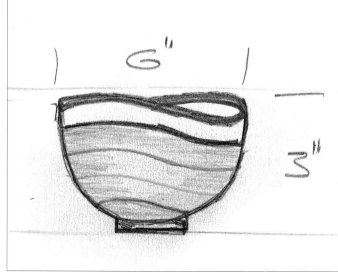

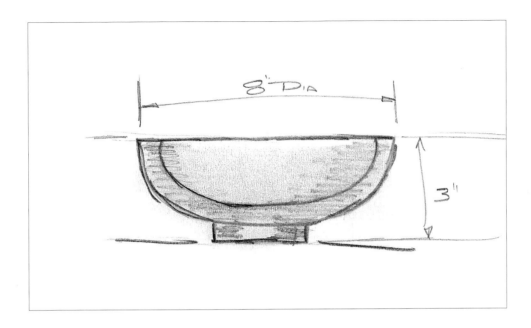

1 Mark out the blank on the log.
2 Cut a slice from the log with a chainsaw.
3 Mark out the blank on the cut slice and cut roughly to shape on the bandsaw.
4 Turn the outside shape, with the bowl held by its top surface on a single-screw chuck. Make the spigot for mounting on the spigot chuck. Your plan should specify the type of chuck to be used: single-screw, faceplate, pin chuck.
5 Turn the inside, with the bowl held by its base in a 2in (51mm) spigot chuck.
6 Finish the area near the base.
7 Wet-sand by hand, using 100, 150 and 240 grits.
8 Part off.
9 Reverse-chuck to finish the base, using wooden jaws mounted on a scroll chuck.
10 Dry the piece for 24 hours in the workshop, then move it into the house.
11 Apply finish to the piece: three coats of lacquer applied by spray.

3 Sizing the blank

The blank has to be larger than the finished bowl to allow for (*a*) cleaning up, (*b*) chucking and tool access, and (*c*) shrinkage while drying.

(*a*) A cleaning-up allowance of ½in (13mm) on the diameter and the same on the length (that is, ¼in (6mm) at either end) should be enough for most situations.

(*b*) Chucking and access allowances depend on the design and the making sequence. A typical sequence would be with the bowl held on the top surface for the first stage of turning, using either a single-screw chuck, a multi-screw chuck or a pin chuck; this would not require any chucking allowance, as the wood to which these chucks fasten is to be turned away in any case.

With the bowl held on a spigot for the second stage, the allowances would be ¼in (6mm) for the spigot, plus a further ¼in (6mm) for parting off – this is twice the thickness of a ⅛in (3mm) parting tool.

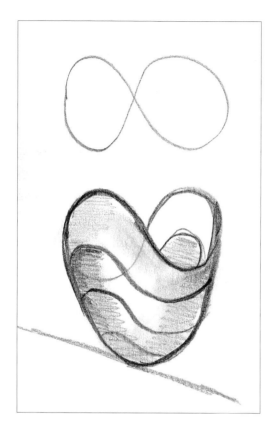

described above. By all means use a waste block if you prefer, but watch that you don't spend more on the glue and the block than the value of the waste material you are trying to save – or even of the whole blank.

(*c*) To allow for shrinkage, increase all dimensions by 10%.

4 Material selection

The qualities of the timber, and possible suitable types of timber, are specified in the design. Taking this together with the size of blanks required, it is just a matter of comparing these requirements with the trees and logs that are available locally and making a selection. Working 'green', the timber should be as fresh as possible, with a moisture content above the fibre saturation point.

It might seem that a fair amount of wood is being wasted in chucking allowances, but that is not true. My view is that we are *saving* the wood in the bowl, and the various allowances permit us to do this. It is no different in principle from the practice of using a waste block to which the blank is glued – if this method is used, then the length of the waste block is the sum of the chucking and access allowances

5 Making the piece

With all the preparation complete and the wood selected, we can now start the making process by following the sequence described in section 2 above. Since all the decisions have been made in advance, the actual making can be tackled with a very positive approach. Lay out all the chucks and tools required for the piece, sharpen the tools, take a good look at the sketch and keep it visible throughout the process.

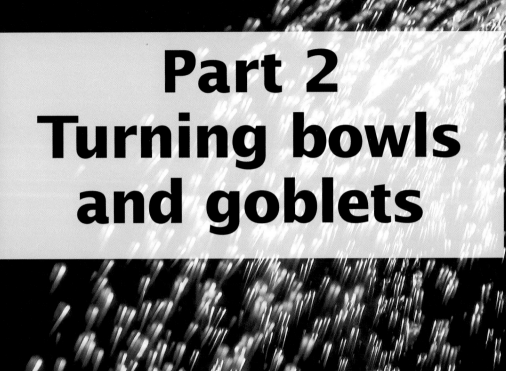

Part 2
Turning bowls and goblets

5 Making shavings

Making shavings is the most exciting part of the whole process. We will now choose some projects and make them by following the plan we have laid out.

The purpose of the exercise is to develop expertise and turning skills in the making of bowls and goblets from green wood. A series of six projects, as detailed below and in Fig 5.1 overleaf, will achieve this:

1 A very thin, translucent cross-grain bowl, 8 x 3¼in (200 x 85mm), ¹⁄₁₆in (1.5mm) thick

2 A thin, natural-edge cross-grain bowl, 6 x 3¼in (150 x 85mm), ⅛in (3mm) thick

3 A thin, translucent end-grain bowl, 5½ x 3½in (140 x 90mm), ⅛in (3mm) thick)

4 A thin, natural-edge end-grain bowl, 5 x 3in (127 x 76mm), ⅛in (3mm) thick

5 A thin, delicate, natural-edge end-grain goblet, 3 x 6in (76 x 152mm), ¹⁄₁₆in (1.5mm) thick

6 A functional bowl made by the part-turning method, 6¼ x 2¾in (159 x 70mm), ⅜in (10mm) thick)

Repetition is one of the best ways of developing manipulative skills, so make at least three of each, but cut 25% more blanks than you need bowls, so that when something goes wrong you have a spare blank ready to use. This saves a lot of worrying about making mistakes and a lot of frustration when things go wrong. I always cut extra blanks and it speeds up my turning.

Timber requirements

The wood characteristics we require for these projects are:

(*a*) Easy to work – there is no point in introducing unnecessary problems, which will slow down the learning process and limit progress.
(*b*) Fresh – preferably less than four weeks from felling.

Additional requirements for the first five projects only:

(*c*) Translucent when thin – this is very useful during the turning process, as it allows us to shine a light through the bowl to provide a visual guide to the wall thickness.
(*d*) For the natural-edge bowls a thin, smooth bark is to be preferred. The wood should be felled in the dormant season to encourage bark retention.

Close-grained hardwoods such as holly, beech, sycamore or maple, in which the sapwood and heartwood are the same colour, will meet all the above requirements, and are ideal.

(*e*) For the last project, the wood should be close-grained, odourless and non-toxic. If possible, it should have low shrinkage rates and the ratio of circumferential to radial shrinkage should be close to 1. This last requirement ensures that distortion is minimal when the piece is remounted after drying. The woods mentioned above, with the exception of holly, would be fine; so would ash, elm, etc.

The rest of the plan for each piece will be covered in the individual chapters below.

Fig 5.1 Six green turning projects

1 Translucent cross-grain bowl
2 Natural-edge cross-grain bowl
3 Translucent end-grain bowl
4 Natural-edge end-grain bowl
5 Natural-edge end-grain goblet
6 Part-turned functional bowl

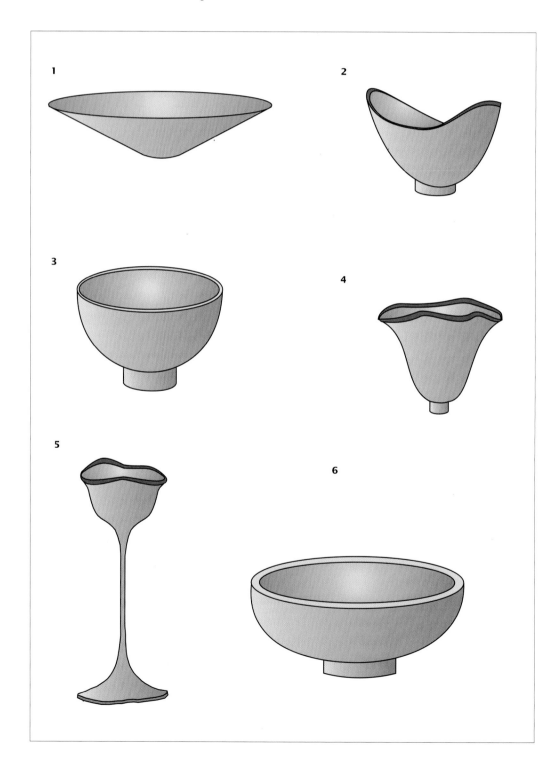

6 Translucent cross-grain bowl

Turning thin, translucent bowls like the one shown in Fig 6.1 is exciting and challenging; the experience will build your confidence for any type of turning, and particularly for the other green turning projects which follow.

1 Design

The shape should be as simple as possible: a shallow V-shape is ideal. The example shown in Fig 6.2 has a finished size of 8in diameter by 3¼in high (200 x 85mm), and is ¹⁄₁₆in (1.5mm) thick.

2 Planning the process

1 Mark out the blanks on the end of the log, having first sawn off a slice about 2in (50mm) thick to get rid of any end cracks.
2 Cut a section 10in (255mm) long with the chainsaw. From this, cut a slice for the bowl blank using either chainsaw or bandsaw. Draw the circle on the slice and cut out the circular blank on the bandsaw.

Fig 6.1 A translucent cross-grain bowl: beginners are advised to start with a reasonably shallow shape

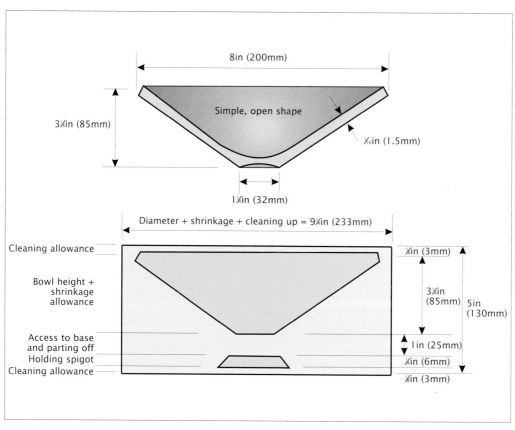

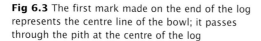

Fig 6.2 Translucent cross-grain bowl: a suitable design for a first green turning project

Fig 6.3 The first mark made on the end of the log represents the centre line of the bowl; it passes through the pith at the centre of the log

3 Turn the outside, holding the bowl on the top with either a single-screw or a multi-screw chuck. Make the spigot for mounting on the second chuck. Use the ½in (13mm) deep-fluted gouge for the whole of this stage.

4 Turn the rim and the inside, holding on the base with a spigot chuck, using the ½in deep-fluted gouge and the 1½in (38mm) round-ended side-cut scraper.

5 Sand by hand, wet, starting with 100-grit down to 240-grit abrasive.

6 Part off with the ⅛in (3mm) parting tool.

7 Sand the base by hand, slightly hollowing the centre.

8 Dry the piece for 24 hours in warm conditions.

9 Apply finish, away from the lathe, by hand or spray.

3 Sizing the blank

(see table at right, and Fig 6.2)

The finished bowl is to be 8 x 3¼in (200 x 85mm).

4 Material selection

We need a piece of close-grained hardwood large enough to make the blanks; it should be fresh, still in the log. Sycamore, holly, beech or maple are all suitable, being easy to turn, light-coloured, and translucent when thin.

5 Making the piece

1 Marking out the blank

First cut off a 2in (50mm) section from the end of the log to remove any splits in the end grain. Pick out the position on the end of the log where you want to make the blank, then draw a centre line for the bowl which goes through the pith
(Fig 6.3). This will ensure an even grain pattern each side. You can then proceed to draw the bowl where you want it around this line, then add on the allowances to make up the bowl blank (Fig 6.4; see also Fig 2.19 on page 22). It doesn't really matter if the pith is included in the allowance for holding, as this material will later be turned away. Having marked out one blank, mark out a second one exactly (or as nearly as possible) the same, so that it will follow the same turning process (Fig 6.5).

2 Cutting the blank

The next thing to do is to cut off a slice from the log about 10in (255mm) long – that is, ¾in (19mm) more than the blank diameter. **Remember the advice concerning chainsaw safety on page 31.**

	Diameter		Height	
	in	mm	in	mm
Bowl size	8	200	3¼	85
Shrinkage allowance, 8–10%	¾	20	¼	8
Cleaning-up allowance:				
Sides	½	13		
Top			⅛	3
Bottom			⅛	3
Parting-off allowance			¼	6
Access allowance			¾	19
Chucking allowance			¼	6
TOTAL	9¼	233	5	130

Fig 6.4 The shape of the bowl marked out on the end of the log, with additional space left below the base of the bowl as a holding allowance

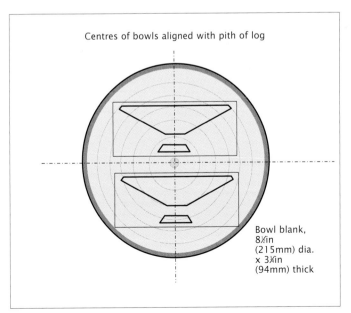

Fig 6.5 Two blanks marked out on log end ready for cutting out

Fig 6.6 The blanks must be aligned with the pith throughout the length of the log to ensure that the pith is not included in the finished bowls. Draw a line through the pith on each end, then join these lines with a chalk line on the outside of the log

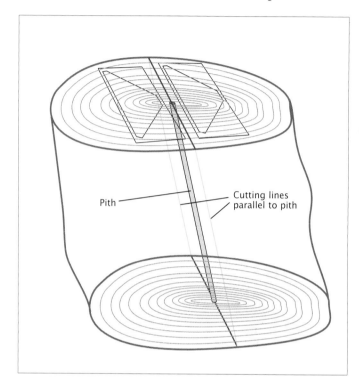

Pith

Cutting lines parallel to pith

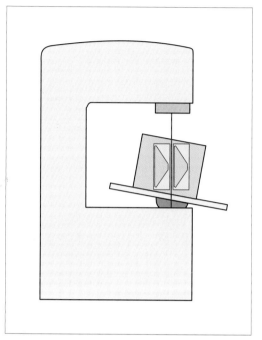

Fig 6.8 Tilting the bandsaw table to ensure that the blade is in line with the pith

Fig 6.7 Drawing datum lines down the side of the log; for convenience, the log has been wedged in position so that the datum lines on the end are vertical

Fig 6.9 The bandsaw blade correctly aligned with the datum line of the side of the log

Examine the other end of the blank to check that the pith is still in the same place and that there are no other defects that would affect the bowl. If, as often happens, the pith has moved to a slightly different position, we must take account of this in slicing up the log; otherwise the pith might run into the bowl.

On the top surface, draw a line through the pith parallel to the tops of the bowls. Then draw a similar line through the pith on the bottom of the log parallel to the line on the top. Join these lines with a chalk mark down the side of the log. This line will be parallel to the pith (Figs 6.6 and 6.7). Align this mark with the bandsaw blade by tilting the table before cutting out the slab (Figs 6.8 and 6.9).

Once the slice has been cut, the circle is drawn on the top surface and the round blank cut out on the bandsaw (Fig 6.10). If the cutting is done accurately there will be no need to true up the blank on the lathe afterwards. All that remains now before mounting the blank on the lathe is to drill a pilot hole for the screw chuck; this is best done with a pillar drill for accuracy (Fig 6.11).

Whatever you do, don't leave the blanks lying around the workshop for a few weeks, or even days, after preparing them, as they are liable to crack due to stresses caused by differential drying. Only cut the blanks you are going to turn on that day – unless you are going to make special storage plans, such as putting them in a plastic bag with wet wood shavings and keeping them in a cool place.

3 Turning the outside

Mount the single-screw chuck on the lathe, then mount the blank on the chuck (Fig 6.12). 1,000rpm will be about the right speed for the lathe, and if the wood is really fresh it will spray sap around the workshop; you need to be aware of this in case there are items around which require protection against the moisture.

The best tool to use for turning is a ½in (13mm) deep-fluted gouge, sharpened with the O'Donnell grind as shown in Chapter 3 (page 34). As the blank is reasonably round and in balance, there should not be any need to spend time truing it up – just get straight into making the bowl shape. To work with the grain on the outside of a cross-grained bowl, the tool should point from the base towards the rim. In this position the tool

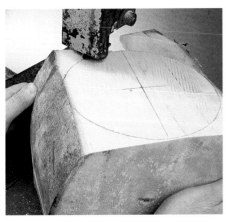

Fig 6.10 The slice has now been cut and the circular outline of the bowl blank drawn on the top of it. This enables an accurate blank to be cut which will not require truing on the lathe

Fig 6.11 Using the pillar drill to bore a pilot hole for the single-screw chuck. Some of the original marking out on the end of the log can still be seen

Fig 6.12 Mounting the prepared blank on the single-screw chuck

will be horizontal (or the handle slightly lowered), and good tool control is achieved as the bevel contact on the wood is behind the cutting edge.

The ideal body position is behind the tool, looking down the bevel, standing in a dynamic stance and ready to 'work away from yourself' (Fig 6.13). I find the Graduate short-bed lathe ideal for this situation, as it gives access all the way around the bowl. On lathes with a long bed and a fixed headstock, the best place to stand is on the opposite side of the long bed, working across it. Swivel-head lathes can be swung to give you the space you need.

The cutting sequence is shown in Figs 6.14–6.20: note how the direction of cutting follows the intended shape right from the first cut. Don't even think about which hand the tool is in – just do it. Make a spigot for the spigot chuck, 2in (51mm) in diameter (or a shallow recess to take a faceplate, if you prefer), and finish by facing off the top surface of the bowl.

Having completed the toolwork on the outside, the bowl can be turned round and held in the second holding position for the inside to be turned (Fig 6.21).

Fig 6.13 Adopt a dynamic stance behind the tool, looking down the bevel

Fig 6.14 Turning the translucent cross-grain bowl: first chucking and cutting sequence

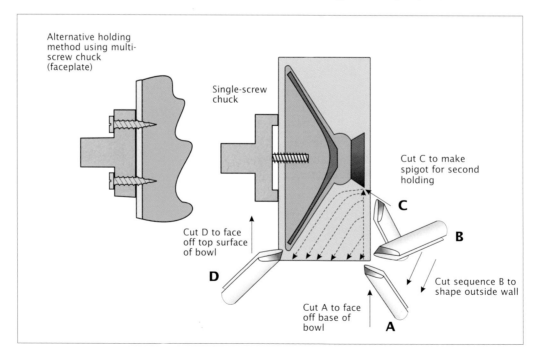

Alternative holding method using multi-screw chuck (faceplate)

Single-screw chuck

Cut C to make spigot for second holding

C

B

Cut D to face off top surface of bowl

Cut sequence B to shape outside wall

D

Cut A to face off base of bowl

A

Fig 6.15 Having faced off the surface which will be the base of the bowl (cut A in Fig 6.14), cut sequence B is begun by chamfering the corner of the blank. Even at this initial stage, the gouge is moving in a direction which follows the intended shape of the bowl

Fig 6.16 As cut sequence B proceeds, the conic profile of the outside rapidly develops

Fig 6.17 While the base of the bowl is still at least 2in (50mm) wide, provision must be made for forming the spigot which will be used for the second chucking. First, the base is trued once more if necessary (*a*), then the internal diameter of the spigot chuck is marked on the wood with dividers (*b*)

a

b

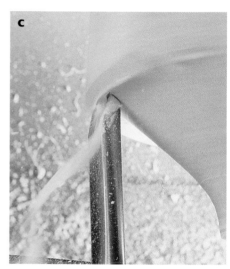
c

Fig 6.18 Cut sequence B can now be completed, leaving untouched the circular area which has been marked out for the spigot

Fig 6.19 Forming the dovetail spigot (cut C)

Fig 6.20 Cut D, facing off the upper surface of the bowl, completes the first chucking

Fig 6.21 Reverse-chucking: mounting the dovetail spigot in the O'Donnell jaws

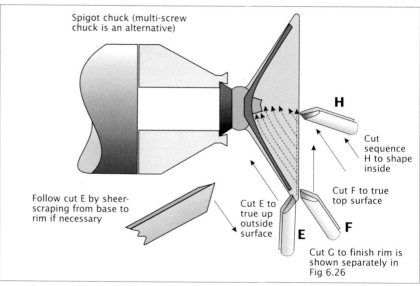

Spigot chuck (multi-screw chuck is an alternative)

H

Cut sequence H to shape inside

Cut F to true top surface

Cut E to true up outside surface

Follow cut E by sheer-scraping from base to rim if necessary

E

F

Cut G to finish rim is shown separately in Fig 6.26

Fig 6.22 Turning the translucent cross-grain bowl: second chucking

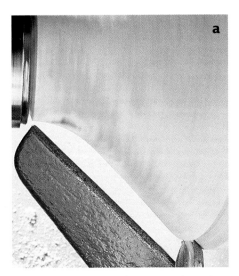

Fig 6.23 A careful cut from rim to base (cut E in Fig 6.22) should be enough to true the outside

Fig 6.24 If cut E has not produced a good finish, sheer-scraping from base to rim will rectify the problem

The next phase of the turning sequence is summarized in Fig 6.22. In theory, if you made a good spigot and you have a good, accurate chuck, then the outside of the bowl will be running true and there is no need to touch it again. In any case, if the bowl is going to be a thick one (more than ¼in (6mm)), a small amount out of true does not matter. But for a thin bowl (less than ¹⁄₁₆in (1.5mm)) even the smallest inaccuracy will be very noticeable, as it will result in an uneven wall thickness – so it is definitely advisable to true the outside now before proceeding further.

Ideally, another cut from the base to the rim should be sufficient to true it up, but in practice there is not room for the tool to approach from this direction. So, with a newly sharpened deep-fluted gouge, make a cut *slowly* and *carefully* from the rim to the base (Fig 6.23); this is necessary to obtain a good finish. Since we are going against the grain here, there is a small risk that this cut will produce a poor finish on some woods; if this does occur, clean up the surface afterwards with a sheer-scraping cut (see pages 40–1), with the tool facing from the base to the rim (Fig 6.24). The

Fig 6.25 Truing the top surface (cut F)

Fig 6.26 Finishing the rim (cut G); the gouge points tangentially around the bowl and is twisted from side to side

top surface is then trued with the deep-fluted gouge (Fig 6.25).

4 Turning the rim and the inside

The rim is next; it is going to be square to the sides, so that the width of the rim is the same as the thickness of the bowl. This is the only cut I make with the tool pointing tangentially around the bowl; heel contact is under the cutting edge, and the tool is twisted to either side from the centre until the rim is a little wider than required (Fig 6.26).

The process of hollowing out the bowl starts in the centre, making each cut follow the final shape (Fig 6.27), just as you did on the outside. If you are doing it right, the tool will be in the opposite hand to that used on the outside. Regular sharpening is necessary, particularly as you come to the last cuts. Never sharpen the gouge for the very last cut because, moving away from your turning stance, you will lose the flow and rhythm you have built up, and coming back will be almost like starting again. It is far better to sharpen the tool when there are two or three cuts left to make, so you have a chance to regain the flow and rhythm.

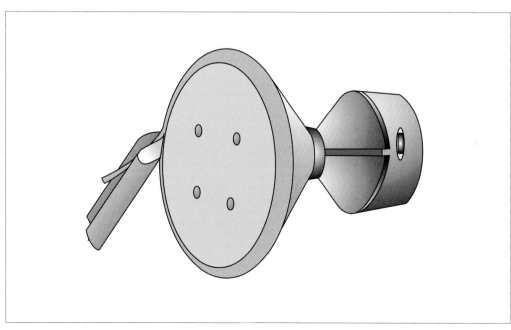

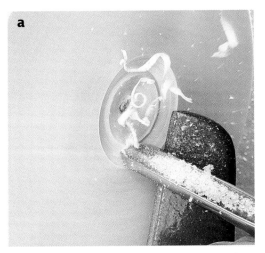

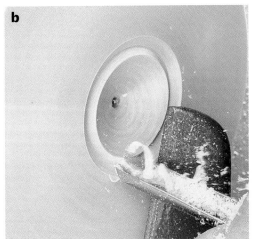

Fig 6.27 Hollowing the inside (cut sequence H)

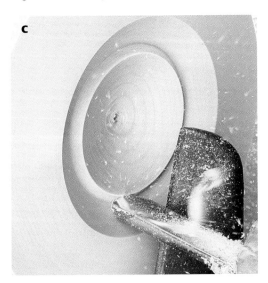

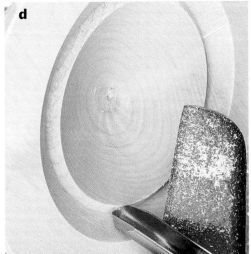

If the bowl is getting dry, water it to keep it moist, **but only if there is no risk of the water coming into contact with the machine's electrics**.

When the wall is about ¾in (19mm) thick, put a lamp behind the bowl so that the light shining through it gives you a visual measure of thickness as the cuts proceed. Again, watch the electrical safety. This is also a good point to start supporting the bowl with your fingers; it will need this support as it gets thinner. The side of the hand is placed on the toolrest, the fingers are on the outside of the bowl and the thumb on top of the gouge. The fingers should be directly supporting the tool through the wood (Fig 6.28). What you

Fig 6.28 A late stage of the hollowing sequence, showing use of fingers to support the bowl (you may prefer to use a glove) and light shining through the bowl wall as a guide to thickness

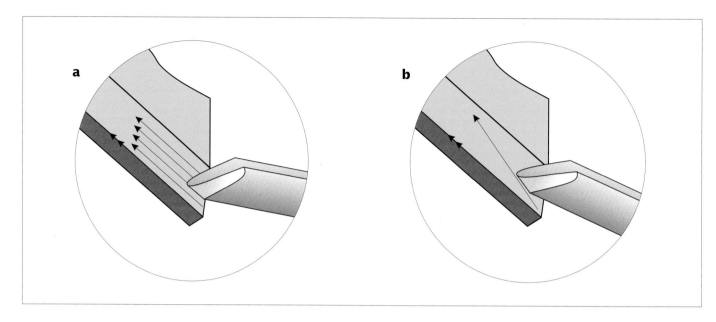

Fig 6.29 Two ways of preparing for the final cut
on the inside

(a) Make a few short cuts of gradually increasing
depth, then take the whole cut in one go

(b) Chamfer the edge of the waste so that the depth
of the final cut will increase gradually

Fig 6.30 Last stage of hollowing: the final 1in
(25mm) is taken in very fine cuts with the deep-
fluted gouge (end of cut sequence H), then
smoothed with the big scraper (cut J) if necessary

have to watch for is the bowl breaking, so a
glove is advisable. You will not be able to
support the bowl with your fingers all the
way down, so as you get to your limit
gradually relax the support hand and take
it away, while the cut continues using the
control hand only (the 'control hand' is the
one holding the handle). The support hand
can then resume support of the tool in the
conventional manner.

Don't leave just a tiny amount to take
off with the last cut, as it is much easier
to take off ⅛in (3mm) or even ¼in (6mm),

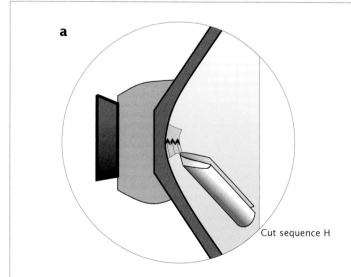

Cut sequence H

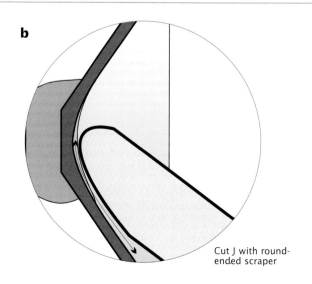

Cut J with round-
ended scraper

Fig 6.31 The final cut in sequence H leaves a small boss in the centre which can then be removed by nibbling with the tip of the gouge

even though you are only leaving a final wall thickness of $\frac{1}{16}$in (1.5mm) or less. You really have to be positive in making these cuts – don't worry if you go right through the first one, as confidence and ability will come with practice. Once you have turned a bowl $\frac{1}{32}$in (0.8mm) thick, then $\frac{1}{8}$in (3mm) will be easy.

Making the entry for the last cut requires care. There are two alternative ways to make it easier. The first is to make a few short, shallow cuts, about $\frac{1}{2}$in (13mm) long, gradually build up to the full depth of the cut and then go right ahead with it (Fig 6.29a) The second is to chamfer the waste in from the edge, then make the start in the normal way (Fig 6.29b). The trickiest bit of all is the centre spot in the bottom: you don't want to rip the grain deeper than the intended shape, or leave a small, annoying pip. For the best results, stop the last two cuts when they are down to 1in (25mm) diameter, then finish the bottom separately, taking fine cuts with the tip of the deep-fluted gouge, making sure that the tip is at centre height as it finishes (Figs 6.30 and 6.31).

If necessary, a big scraper can be used to clean up in the bottom of the bowl (Fig 6.32), but don't bring it all the way up the side to the rim, as there is a high risk of shattering the bowl. Sheer-scraping with hand support will improve the finish and reduce risks.

Fig 6.32 Cleaning the inside with the round-ended scraper (cut J)

Fig 6.33 Sanding inside and out with cloth-backed abrasive

5 Sanding

Most of the bowl is now finished and ready for sanding, which is best done before we finish the base. Wet-sand with 100 to 240 grit, as described on page 42 (Fig 6.33).

The outside of the base, which was previously left heavy so as to give sufficient strength to turn the inside, can now be finish-turned with the deep-fluted gouge (Figs 6.34 and 6.35); sand this area separately.

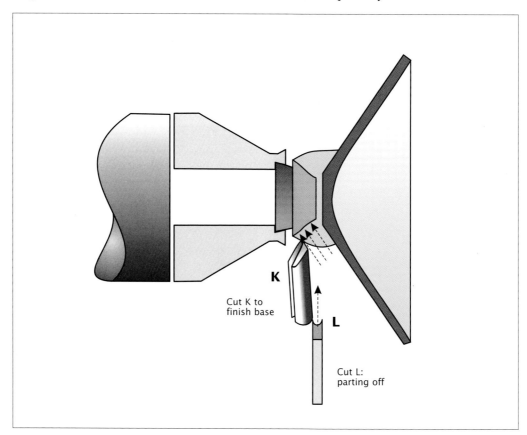

K
Cut K to finish base

L
Cut L: parting off

Fig 6.34 Finishing around the base and parting off

Fig 6.35 Finishing the foot of the bowl (cut K)

6 Parting off

Part off with the ⅛in (3mm) parting tool in the left hand, while the right hand is callipered round the bowl ready to catch it as soon as it is separated (Fig 6.36).

7 Finishing the base

This leaves only the bottom to be finished. Use a hand scraper to create a hollow in the centre, then sand the centre and the edge by hand. Alternatively, if you want to turn the underside of the base, mount it in the wood jaws of a scroll chuck and clean up the base with the deep-fluted gouge, followed by sanding.

8 Drying

As this piece is very thin, there should be no problem with putting it into warm conditions straight away; it could be dry in a couple of hours.

9 Applying finish

This is a decorative bowl, for which I prefer to use a hard finish. Spray on three coats of Craftlac melamine as described on page 43.

Conclusion

It is not just the turning technique that is important in a project like this, but the whole process you have been through, and the best way to progress is to repeat it again and again. Try working in small batches, doing all the outsides then all the insides, and don't worry if one or two of them go wrong – just get on with the next. This practice will stand you in good stead for the following projects.

Fig 6.36 Parting off (cut L)

7 Natural-edge cross-grain bowl

1 Design

This is a simple natural-bark-edged bowl with only a little rise and fall of the rim. It is evenly balanced, with the two high points the same height, as are the two low points – altogether a very pleasing shape, and the shape we should be aiming for (Fig 7.1). It is a little smaller than the previous flat-topped bowl, as it presents different difficulties: dimensions of 6in (150mm) diameter x 3¼in (85mm) high and ⅛in (3mm) thick will be challenging enough.

2 Planning the process

Because we have a natural top, there are several alternative chucking sequences to be considered:

1 The first possibility is to put a faceplate on the bottom of the blank and complete all the turning operations before parting it off. This is a relatively simple procedure, but control over the balance of the rim is difficult, as it is dictated by the accuracy of your

Fig 7.1 A simple, balanced shape is best for your first natural-edge bowl

marking out, as well as of the chainsaw and bandsaw work. The position of the faceplate will also be critical. Avoid this method.

2 The second option is to put the bowl between centres on the lathe with the drive centre in the top surface, having first drilled away the bark at this point to give the drive dog a firm grip. Once it is correctly aligned, the tailstock can be tightened up and the outside of the bowl is ready for turning. The great advantage with this method is that there is very good control over rim alignment, which is particularly important with a design of this nature. The disadvantage is that the tailstock restricts access and hampers tool technique during the initial turning.

3 The method I prefer is to hold the bowl on a pin chuck while the outside is turned and the base prepared for the second chucking. In this case the hole for the pin chuck becomes a datum for the alignment of the rim, so great care should be taken in the drilling of the hole. Once fixed on the pin chuck, the bowl is very secure, and there is plenty of access all around the bowl for turning as we do not need the tailstock – in fact it is probably better to take the tailstock off the lathe at this point so that it doesn't get in the way of the tool handles.

If option **2** or **3** is chosen for the first holding, the second holding method would be a 2in (51mm) spigot.

For this project I am using the pin chuck.

1 Mark out the blank on the timber.
2 Cut the slice from the log with a chainsaw.
3 Cut the blank round on the bandsaw.
4 Drill 1½in (38mm) hole for a pin chuck. Turn the outside, holding on the pin chuck. Make spigot for second holding.
5 Turn the inside, holding in a spigot chuck.
6 Sand by hand, wet.
7 Part off.
8 Reverse-chuck between centres to finish base, if required.
9 Dry the piece for 3–4 days in a cool, humid atmosphere.
10 Apply finish to the piece.

3 Sizing the blank

Having chosen a chucking sequence, you can work out the allowances; these will be much the same as for the first exercise, but with no need for a top-cleaning allowance. Refer to the table, below left.

4 Material selection

The design specifies all the necessary requirements for the bowl, so all that is required is to find a log of suitable size and type so that the bowl can be made. The bark should be thin and in good condition, and at least one side of the log should be a suitable shape to give an even, gentle rise and fall to the rim. As before, suitable timbers include sycamore, holly, beech and maple.

	Diameter		Height	
	in	mm	in	mm
Bowl size	6	150	3¼	85
Shrinkage allowance, 8–10%	½	15	¼	6
Cleaning-up allowance:				
Sides	½	13		
Top			0	0
Bottom			¼	6
Parting-off allowance			¼	6
Access allowance			¾	19
Chucking allowance			¼	6
TOTAL	7	178	5	128

5 Making the piece

1 Marking out the blank

Cut a slice, about 2in (50mm) wide, off the end to clear any small cracks; but make sure that the spikes of the chainsaw, which grip into the log to give you control, are on the waste side of the chain, otherwise they could destroy a number of bowls. Transfer the bowl design to the log and add on all the allowances to give the blank size (Figs 7.2 and 7.3; see also Fig 2.19 on page 22).

2 Cutting the blank

The next chainsaw cut is to take a slice off the log 8in (200mm) wide – 1in (25mm) wider than the diameter of the bowl – again watching the position of the spikes (Fig 7.4).

3 Shaping the blank

This next stage is where a bandsaw with a large depth of cut is invaluable; it will do the rest of the cutting much more

accurately than the chainsaw. Draw the datum line C in Fig 2.19 (page 22), which ensures that the two low points on the rim are at the same level. We also want the two high points to be the same height, which means that the base line has to be cut parallel with the two peaks. This is arranged by putting the block of wood on the bandsaw table and lining up the peaks against the bandsaw blade, then adjusting the tilt of the table until both peaks touch

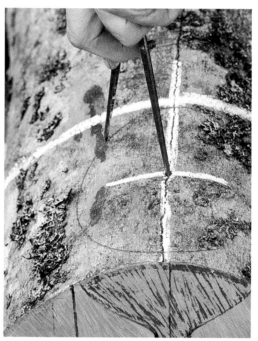

Fig 7.3 Marking out the shape of the bowl on the side of the log. The diameter of the bowl, plus cleaning allowance, has first been marked on the bark in white chalk

Fig 7.2 The bowl shape, and the holding allowance below the base, marked on the end of the log

Fig 7.4 Sawing along the uppermost chalk line in the previous photograph produces a slice just a little thicker than the intended diameter of the bowl

the blade at the same time (Figs 7.5 and 7.6). The table should be locked in this position while the cut is made along the base of the blank (Fig 7.7).

If you have not done so already, carefully draw the circle on the bark surface, then, after returning the bandsaw table to the horizontal position, cut out the circular blank (Fig 7.8). Each step you make reveals a little more of the finished bowl. If you have cut reasonably accurately, then the flow of the bark edge on the blank will be close to the shape that the finished edge is going to be on the bowl.

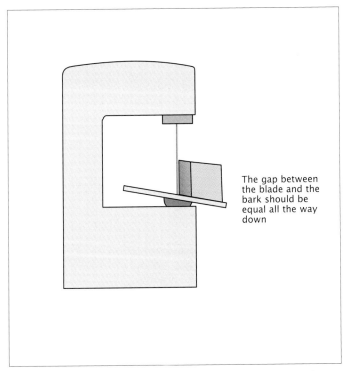

The gap between the blade and the bark should be equal all the way down

Fig 7.5 Adjusting the tilt of the bandsaw table so the top edge of the bowl is parallel to the blade

Fig 7.7 Cutting along the base of the blank with the bandsaw, leaving a generous holding allowance below the base of the bowl itself

Fig 7.6 The log section correctly aligned with the bandsaw blade. The white chalk marks on the bark indicate the maximum diameter of the bowl

Fig 7.8 Cutting out the circular blank, with the bandsaw table horizontal

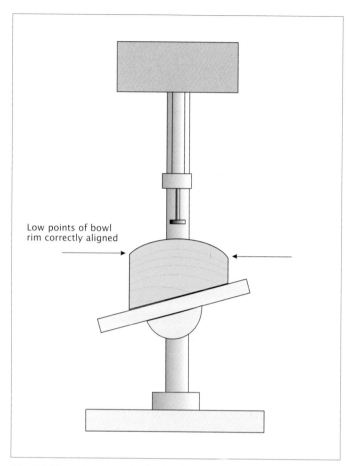

Fig 7.9 Mounting on a pin chuck: aligning the rim by tilting the table of the pillar drill before boring the hole

Fig 7.10 Mounting on a pin chuck: (*a*) using a try square to align the high points; (*b*) checking the alignment of the low points by eye

Fig 7.11 Using a Forstner bit in the drill press to bore an accurate hole for the pin chuck

4 Turning the outside

The final alignment of the rim is made on the pillar drill by tilting the table and aligning the rim with the pillar before drilling the hole for the pin chuck (Figs 7.9 and 7.10). Drill the 1½in (38mm) hole 1½in deep with a sawtooth or Forstner bit (Fig 7.11), then mount the blank on the lathe. Remove the tailstock from the lathe, if possible, to give plenty of clear space.

If you prefer to hold between centres, drill away the bark at the centre with a 1in (25mm) drill – the same diameter as your drive centre, or larger – so as to give a positive location for the drive centre. Mount the blank lightly between centres

Fig 7.12 Mounting between centres: the blank is rotated by hand to check that (*a*) the high points and (*b*) the low points of the rim are level

and spin it slowly by hand so that you can judge the balance of the rim (7.12). What you are aiming for is for the two high spots on the rim to be the same height, and also the two low spots. This balance can be adjusted as necessary by moving the position of the tailstock centre in the blank. The turning process will be much the same as for the pin chuck

method, except that access around the tailstock will be a little more awkward.

Set the speed at about 1,200rpm and again take a ½in (13mm) deep-fluted gouge as the turning tool; then we are ready to turn.

Fig 7.13 Turning the natural-edge cross-grain bowl: first chucking

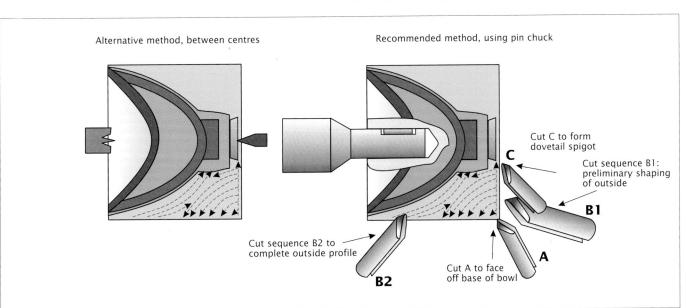

Alternative method, between centres

Recommended method, using pin chuck

Cut C to form dovetail spigot

C

Cut sequence B1: preliminary shaping of outside

B1

Cut sequence B2 to complete outside profile

B2

Cut A to face off base of bowl

A

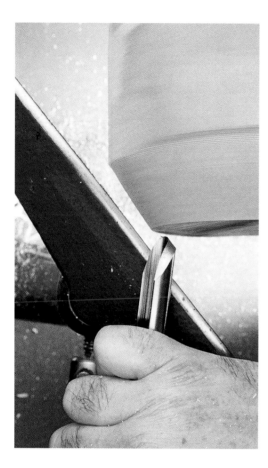

Fig 7.14 The bottom surface of the blank having been faced off (cut A in Fig 7.13), cut sequence B1 is begun by chamfering the corner

The cutting sequence for shaping the outside is shown in Figs 7.13–7.20. As with all cross-grain bowls, the correct way to turn the outside, in order to be cutting with the grain, is to work with the tool facing from the small diameter to the large. This causes no problems while we are cutting the initial shape in the solid wood (cut sequence B1), but once the cut begins to approach the bark edge from underneath there is a risk of the bark being pushed off by the gouge. Therefore, when cutting in the bark area, and particularly when approaching the final shape, the cuts have to be made from the rim to the base instead (cut sequence B2 in Fig 7.13, and Fig 7.20). Although this cut will be going against the grain, the finish will be good on green wood providing the tool is sharp and the cut is taken slowly and carefully.

Fig 7.15 A series of fluid cuts, following the shape of the foot and the bowl wall, brings the profile to an ogee shape

Fig 7.16 It is important for cut sequence B1 to stop short of the rim area, to avoid the danger of knocking off the bark

Fig 7.17 Cleaning up the base prior to forming the dovetail spigot

Fig 7.18 Forming the dovetail spigot (cut C). The required diameter is measured from the jaws of the chuck using dividers (*a*), the marks reinforced in pencil (*b*), and the cut made with the flute of the gouge facing away from the operator (*c*)

Fig 7.19 The last cut in sequence B1 reduces the diameter of the base to only slightly more than that of the dovetail spigot

The new dimension in turning a natural edge is that the rim is intermittent, which makes it more difficult to see, particularly when turning the inside. To improve visibility, clear the wood shavings from the lathe bed and mount a piece of rigid white plastic or card there, in your line of sight of the bowl. Adjust the lighting position to give the best visibility of your intermittent edge – the difference can be dramatic (Fig 7.21).

Once the spigot has been prepared for the next holding, the bowl can be taken off the lathe and turned round (Fig 7.22). The chucking sequence for the second holding is shown in Fig 7.23.

As in the previous project, make a final pass down the outside with the bowl held on its base to ensure that it is running absolutely true (Fig 7.24). Then, if necessary, sheer-scrape up the outside to get the final finish (Fig 7.25).

Fig 7.20 Finishing cuts are made from rim to base (sequence B2) to avoid dislodging the bark

Fig 7.21 A view of the bowl at a later stage (after completion of cut E), showing how a white background improves visibility of the intermittent edge

Fig 7.22 The bowl remounted, with the dovetail spigot installed in the O'Donnell jaws

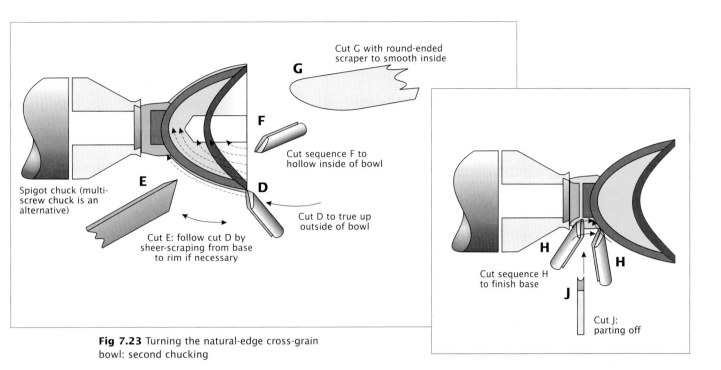

Cut G with round-ended
scraper to smooth inside

G

F

Cut sequence F to
hollow inside of bowl

Spigot chuck (multi-
screw chuck is an
alternative)

E

D

Cut D to true up
outside of bowl

Cut E: follow cut D by
sheer-scraping from base
to rim if necessary

Cut sequence H
to finish base

H   **H**

J

Cut J:
parting off

Fig 7.23 Turning the natural-edge cross-grain
bowl: second chucking

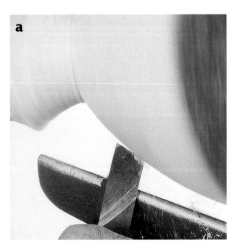
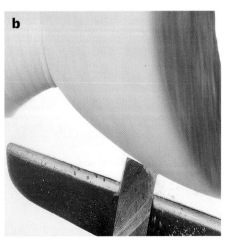

Fig 7.24 Truing the outside after rechucking (cut D)

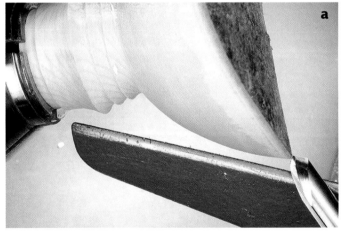

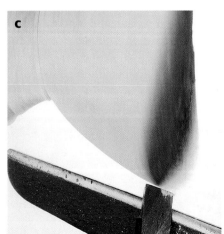

Fig 7.25 Sheer-scraping from base to rim to produce the final finish on the outside (cut E)

5 Turning the inside

Turn the inside as before, starting in the middle and working the finished shape until you come down to the right thickness, in this case ⅛in (3mm). Place a light behind the bowl to gauge the thickness; in the area where the rim is intermittent, the actual wall thickness can be seen (Fig 7.26). If you used a pin chuck for the previous stage, roughing out the inside is much easier and quicker, since much of the centre of the bowl – the last and most difficult part of each cut – has already been removed.

Again my preference is to make all the cuts from rim to base in one sweep, following the final shape each time until the desired thickness is achieved. Use hand support on the outside as before – but a little more care will be needed this time, because there can be problems with the stability of the intermittent natural edge as it gets thin (Fig 7.27).

Alternatively, once the thickness is down to ½in (13mm) overall, continue turning just the rim section to the final thickness. Then the remainder of the inside can be turned as if it were an ordinary bowl, and the final cut blended into the rim (Fig 7.28). Any tidying up with a big scraper in the bottom of the bowl is fine (Fig 7.29), but bringing the scraper up close to the natural edge can be risky.

a

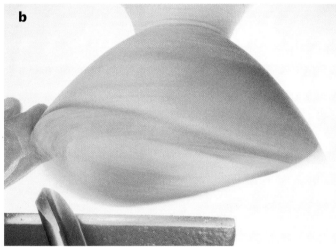

b

c

Fig 7.27 Stages in hollowing the inside (cut sequence F), using hand support as the wall thickness diminishes

Fig 7.26 With a strong light placed behind the bowl, the wall thickness can be seen clearly where the rim is intermittent

Fig 7.28 The final stages of cut sequence F: blending the lower part of the interior into the already thinned rim

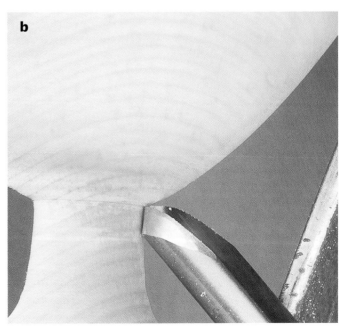

Fig 7.29 Tidying the bottom of the bowl with the round-ended scraper (cut G). It is not advisable to use this near the fragile rim

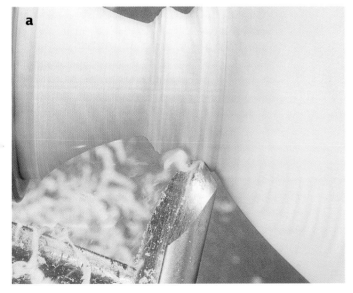

Fig 7.30 The foot is shaped by cutting alternately (*a*) towards and (*b*) along the stem (cut H)

Fig 7.31 Hand-sanding inside and out

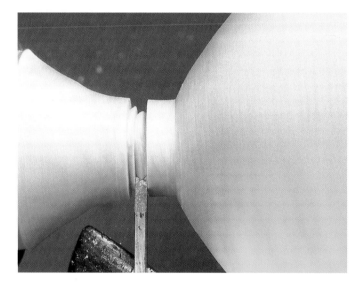

Fig 7.32 Parting off. If you are afraid of dropping the bowl, stop the lathe and use a saw to separate the last ¼in (6mm)

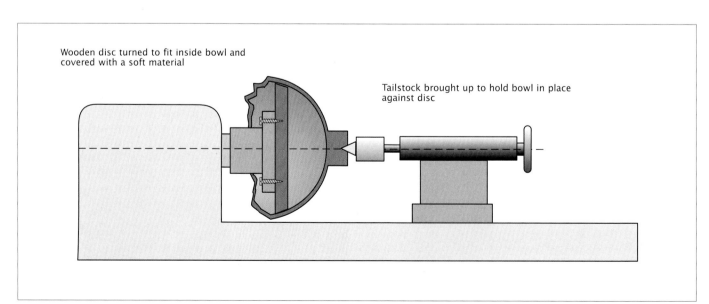

Wooden disc turned to fit inside bowl and covered with a soft material

Tailstock brought up to hold bowl in place against disc

Fig 7.33 A method of reverse-chucking the bowl if further finishing of the foot is required

I prefer to sand the rest of the bowl before finishing the foot area as for the previous project (Fig 7.30).

6 Sanding

The bowl is hand-sanded, wet, on the lathe, inside and out (Fig 7.31), as described on page 42.

7 Parting off

The last operation is parting off (Fig 7.32). Just in case I don't manage to catch the bowl, I always part off down to ¼in (6mm) diameter, stop the lathe, and take a small handsaw for the final parting off. Once dry, the bottom can be made flat and hollow with a hand scraper.

8 Reverse-chucking

If you wish to turn the underside of the base further, then reverse-chucking is required. The process is a little different from that used with the flat-rimmed bowls, as this time we do not have a solid edge to grip. The procedure is to turn a disc with its edge following the same shape as the inside of the bowl at the point where it is likely to touch, and cover this with a soft, thin material to avoid marking the inside of the bowl. The bowl is placed over this and the tailstock brought up to hold it in place. Final turning of the base can then be completed (7.33).

9 Drying

As this piece is thicker than the previous project, dry it a little more slowly – say 3–4 days in cool, humid conditions, then into the house.

10 Applying finish

Finish as described on page 43.

8 Translucent end-grain bowl

Changing the grain orientation in bowl making from cross grain to end grain is like starting again: different grain patterns, different turning methods, different sequencing, as well as different planning and timber preparation – in fact it is a whole new way of making bowls and vessels. Having got used to the rituals of making cross-grain bowls, I found the change to end-grain turning very refreshing.

1 Design

A bowl about 5½in (140mm) diameter by 3½in (90mm) tall and ⅛in (3mm) thick is a good size to start with, and this time we are going for a rounded shape (Fig 8.1).

Fig 8.1 A flat-rimmed bowl turned end-grain: the procedures are quite different from those used for cross-grain bowls

2 Planning the process

1 Mark out the length of the blank on the log.
2 Cut the log to length with the chainsaw, bandsaw or bush saw.
3 Hold between centres to clean up the log, rough out the bowl blank and prepare the face for the multi-screw chuck (faceplate).
4 Hold the bowl on the base with the faceplate to turn the outside.
5 Turn the inside, still on the faceplate.
6 Sand.
7 Part off.
8 Reverse-chuck to finish the base, using wooden jaw plates in the scroll chuck.
9 Dry the piece for 4–5 days in cool conditions.
10 Apply finish.

	Diameter		Height	
	in	mm	in	mm
Bowl size (1)	5½	140	3½	90
Shrinkage allowance, 8–10%	½	14	0	0
Cleaning-up allowance:				
Sides	½	12		
Top			½	12
Bottom			¼	6
Parting-off allowance			¼	6
Access allowance			½	12
Chucking allowance (2)			1¼	32
TOTAL	6½	166	6¼	158

Notes:
(1) These dimensions are excluding bark.
(2) Chucking allowance assumes use of 1in (25mm) faceplate with screws penetrating ¾in (19mm) into the wood.

3 Sizing the blank

Taking into account the bark and the irregularity of the shape, we will need a branch of around 7–7½in (180–190mm) diameter and 6¼in (158mm) long. Refer to the table, above right.

4 Material selection

Timber selection is made on a similar basis as for the cross-grain bowls: fresh, close-grained and easy to turn, with no difference in appearance between heart and sapwood, and translucent when thin. Take a clean, short log, just larger than the size required, and the blank is virtually prepared.

This aspect of end-grain work appeals to me, as we can work with small logs or branches and it is only a few minutes from the log to the lathe. Doing it this way, inevitably the pith will be in the centre of the bowl, and heart defects such as localized cracks around the pith could limit your choice of timber. While it might be possible to fill, glue and smooth these out on the finished piece, the effort is not worth it, and usually they will still look like filled cracks – but for a practice piece it doesn't really matter.

5 Making the piece

1 Marking out the blank

Mark the position of the finished bowl on one end of the branch, and identify this end as the top. Then mark the length of the blank.

2 Cutting the blank

Use the chainsaw, bandsaw or bush saw, as convenient, to cut the log to the required length.

Fig 8.2 The blank marked and sawn to the appropriate length, with a centre mark on each end – no further preparation is required before mounting on the lathe

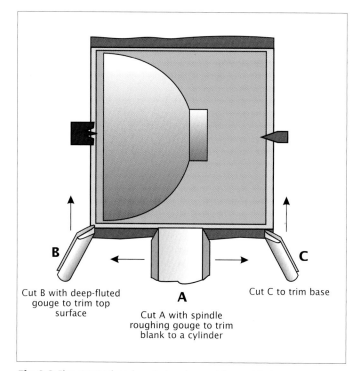

B — Cut B with deep-fluted gouge to trim top surface

A — Cut A with spindle roughing gouge to trim blank to a cylinder

C — Cut C to trim base

Fig 8.3 Flat-rimmed end-grain bowl: roughing out between centres

Fig 8.4 Trimming the log to a cylinder with the spindle roughing gouge (cut A)

Fig 8.5 Trimming the base to a slightly concave surface with the deep-fluted gouge to ensure a close fit around the rim of the multi-screw chuck (cut C)

Draw a circle on each end of the log to find the centre. Re-mark which end is going to be the top of the bowl (Fig 8.2).

3 Roughing out the blank

Hold the branch between centres, with the 'top' at the headstock end; this gives better access to clean up and level the base and prepare for the next holding (Fig 8.3). With the speed at around 1,200rpm, trim up the blank with the 1¼in (32mm) spindle roughing gouge (Fig 8.4), then square both ends with a deep-fluted gouge ready for fitting a faceplate to the base. Make the base very slightly concave to ensure that the blank is supported around the rim of the multi-screw chuck (Fig 8.5). To give yourself a guide for centring the faceplate, draw a few pencil lines at about the right diameter while the blank is rotating (Fig 8.6).

Fig 8.6 Concentric circles pencilled on the base of the blank (*a*) serve as a useful guide when fitting the faceplate (*b*)

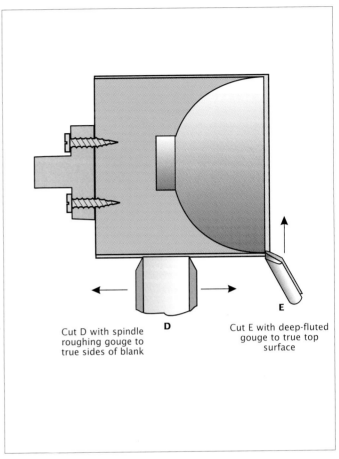

Cut D with spindle roughing gouge to true sides of blank

Cut E with deep-fluted gouge to true top surface

Fig 8.7 Flat-rimmed end-grain bowl: truing up the blank after remounting on the multi-screw chuck (faceplate)

4 Turning the outside

Once the blank is mounted on the faceplate, the chances are that it will be running slightly out of true, but *do not* bring up the tailstock to the previous centre, as this could put extra strain on the screws. You really have to have confidence in your chosen holding method, so the tailstock is best removed from the lathe altogether – then it won't get in the way of the tool and your arm. Trim up the outside again with the spindle roughing gouge and take a fine cut across the end face with the deep-fluted gouge to clean up the rim surface (Figs 8.7 and 8.8).

There is a convention in bowl-turning procedure that on end-grain bowls the *inside* is turned and finished first. Until

Fig 8.8 Truing the outside after remounting the blank on the multi-screw chuck (faceplate), with the tailstock removed to improve access

recently, I always followed this convention, and it produced the goods; but it makes life a little difficult on some end-grain work, since the shape of the bowl is first determined on the inside, where you don't have a good view of it. It was this difficulty that led me to do larger end-grain bowls the other way round, and the difference was dramatic: it almost halved the time taken, and the shapes were much better.

The convention arose in connection with objects like goblets where, if the outside shape was done first, there would be no strength in the stem to enable the inside to be turned. Turning the outside first is fine, providing you leave enough holding wood to ensure sufficient strength while turning the inside.

When turning the outside first, the next step is to mark the height of the bowl

Fig 8.9 The bowl blank trued up, with the height of the bowl marked in pencil

Fig 8.10 Flat-rimmed end-grain bowl: first stages in shaping the bowl

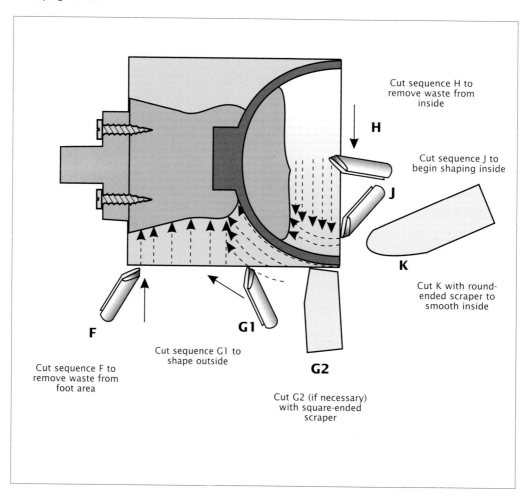

Cut sequence H to remove waste from inside

H

Cut sequence J to begin shaping inside

J

K

Cut K with round-ended scraper to smooth inside

F

Cut sequence F to remove waste from foot area

Cut sequence G1 to shape outside

G1

G2

Cut G2 (if necessary) with square-ended scraper

Fig 8.11 Removing the waste from the foot area with the deep-fluted gouge (cut sequence F)

(excluding the foot) down from the rim (Fig 8.9). This gives a valuable visual guide to what you are making, and where it is in the block. The waste can then be removed with the deep-fluted gouge, as shown by cut sequence F in Fig 8.10, and Fig 8.11.

Now use the deep-fluted gouge to shape the outside, working as usual from the large diameter to the small (cut sequence G1; Fig 8.12). The whole of the final shape is best made in one sweep from the rim to the base; this will give a much cleaner curve. With a bit of luck this should be right first time; if it is not, take the large square scraper and trim it up to finish the outside (cut G2; Fig 8.13).

Fig 8.12 Shaping the outside with the deep-fluted gouge (cut sequence G1)

Fig 8.13 The outside is cleaned up if necessary with the square-ended scraper (cut G2)

Fig 8.14 Removing waste from the inside by drawing the deep-fluted gouge across the end of the bowl (cut sequence H)

Fig 8.15 Refining the inside by cutting from rim towards base (cut sequence J)

5 Turning the inside

If you are on a lathe with a rotating headstock, a few degrees of swing will give you better access for hollowing out the bowl. To cut with the grain when working on the inside of an end-grain bowl, the tool should be facing from the small diameter to the large; but with conventional gouges, doing this and having bevel control at the same time is not possible. Instead, turn the inside in two stages so that there is more strength in the bowl while finishing up to the rim. First remove the bulk of the wood by drawing the deep-fluted gouge across the bowl (cut sequence H and Fig 8.14), which is a lighter cut than pushing into the end grain. This procedure will take out most of the waste efficiently, but the shape and finish will be crude. Refine the shape with cut sequence J (Fig 8.15); then final shaping should be done with a very

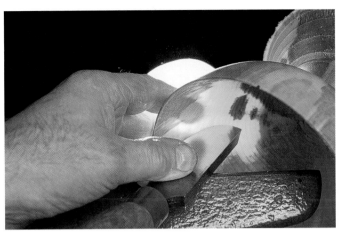

Fig 8.16 Final shaping of the inside with the rounded-ended scraper, using hand support near the rim (cut K)

large, long-handled, round-end side-cut scraper, with hand support to the wall near the rim (cut K; Fig 8.16). This procedure will then need to be repeated (cut sequences L and M in Fig 8.17; cut N in Fig 8.18) in order to bring the inside to its full depth.

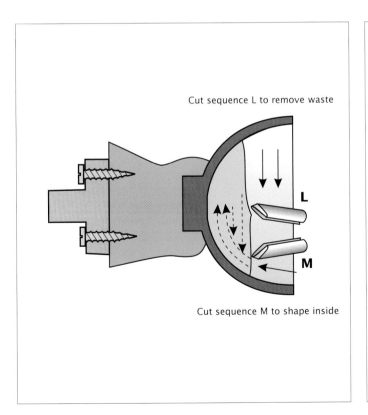

Fig 8.17 Flat-rimmed end-grain bowl: later stages in shaping the inside

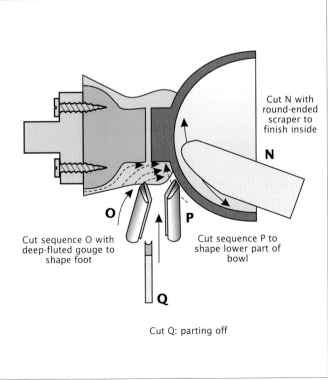

Fig 8.18 Flat-rimmed end-grain bowl: final stages of faceplate turning

Fig 8.19 Wet-sanding inside and out. Take care not to let water come in contact with any electrical components

Fig 8.20 Shaping the foot by cutting alternately (*a*) along and (*b*) towards the foot (cut sequences O and P)

Fig 8.21 Parting off (cut Q)

An alternative approach which can be used for hollowing is to cut from the rim to the base, as you would on a cross-grain bowl, then finish off in the bottom with the large scraper. Ring tools can be used to hollow end-grain bowls, cutting with the grain, but I find that using a deep-fluted gouge and a scraper is faster and gives better control over the form.

6 Sanding

Wet-sand at this stage, both inside and out, while there is still a certain amount of waste wood around the foot to provide stability (Fig 8.19).

The foot is shaped, as in the previous project, by cutting alternately along and towards the foot with the deep-fluted gouge (cut sequences O and P; Fig 8.20).

7 Parting off

Use the ⅛in (3mm) parting tool (cut Q in Fig 8.18, and Fig 8.21). Take care when catching the bowl, or the last few fibres may rip back into the base.

8 Reverse-chucking

A third holding on the external wooden jaws is needed (Figs 8.22 and 8.23) to finish the base with the deep-fluted

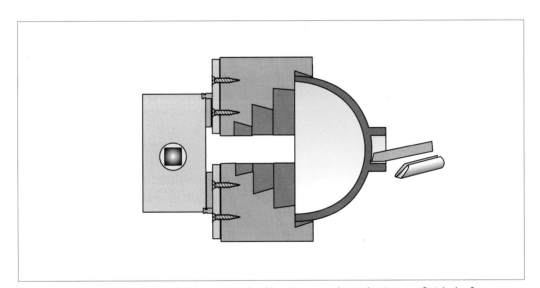

Fig 8.22 Flat-rimmed end-grain bowl: reverse-chucking in external wooden jaws to finish the foot

Fig 8.23 Mounting the bowl in the external wooden jaws

Fig 8.24 Stages in finishing the foot: (*a*) truing the outside with the deep-fluted gouge; the underside has already been faced off and a pencil mark drawn on to indicate the inside diameter; (*b*) hollowing with the deep-fluted gouge; (*c*) finishing with the square-ended side-cut scraper

gouge and the square-ended side-cut scraper (Fig 8.24), taking care to follow through the curve of the bowl inside the base. This will reduce the risk of splitting around the pith. It also gives the bowl a finished and professional look (Fig 8.25). Wet-sand the base.

9 Drying

Dry slowly, for 4–5 days in cool conditions.

10 Applying finish

Apply the finish as described on page 43.

Fig 8.25 A neatly hollowed foot (here receiving its final sanding) gives the bowl a finished and refined appearance

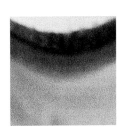

9 Natural-edge end-grain bowl

I like end-grain natural-edge bowls for their simplicity in form, preparation and turning; they are a small step on from the flat-topped end-grain bowl, with some difference in procedure and technique, particularly around the rim (Fig 9.1).

1 Design

The design of the rim – which will be the widest part of an end-grain bowl, since it is formed by the outer surface of the log – is linked to the shape of the log, as we discussed in Chapter 2 (pages 21–4): the more irregular the log section is, the more interesting the rim shape. Don't be too ambitious with the log shape at first, as this could lead to unnecessary difficulties. Try a branch which is slightly irregular in section, square to oval, about 4½–5in (115–125mm) in diameter for a bowl about 3in (75mm) tall.

Fig 9.1 The natural-edge end-grain bowl uses similar techniques to the previous project

2 Planning the process

1 Cut the blank to length from the log with a bush saw, chainsaw or bandsaw.
2 Find and mark the centre at each end of the log.
3 Hold between centres to rough out the blank, balance the piece and turn a spigot for the second holding.
4 Hold on the base with a spigot chuck to turn and sand the inside.
5 Turn the outside: hold as for inside. Sand at each stage.
6 Part off.
7 Dry the piece for 2–3 days in cool conditions.
8 Apply finish.

Fig 9.2 The log cut to length. This log is somewhat triangular in section, and compasses have been used to mark the centre from the three corners of the triangle

3 Sizing the blank

The log should be 5in (127mm) long if you are using a spigot chuck, or 5½in (140mm) if you use a multi-screw chuck.

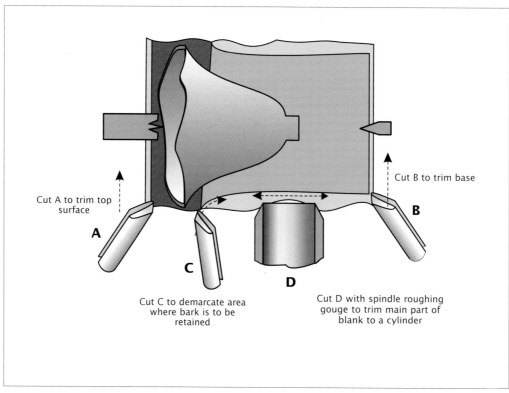

Cut A to trim top surface

A

Cut B to trim base

B

Cut C to demarcate area where bark is to be retained

C

Cut D with spindle roughing gouge to trim main part of blank to a cylinder

D

Fig 9.3 Natural-edge end-grain bowl: roughing out between centres

4 Material selection

Since the bark is to be part of the finished bowl, it should be in good condition with no surface blemishes in the area where the rim is to be. Other requirements are as specified in the design.

5 Making the piece

1 Cutting the blank

Select your log and cut it to length with the chainsaw or bandsaw as convenient.

2 Marking the centre

Find and mark the centre at each end of the log, and put an identifying mark on the top end (Fig 9.2).

3 Roughing out the blank

The purpose of this first mounting (Fig 9.3) is to prepare the blank for the second mounting by facing up the top end, taking out some of the imbalance and making a spigot.

Mount the log lightly between centres with the bowl rim at the headstock end (Fig 9.4). The balance of the rim can be checked by spinning the blank by hand, and the position of the drive centre adjusted as necessary. Then tighten up the tailstock and set the lathe speed to about 1,200rpm. Clean up the top and bottom ends of the log with the deep-fluted gouge (cuts A and B in Fig 9.3, and Fig 9.5), then make a chalk mark about 1in (25mm) from the top to indicate where the rim is going to be, so you don't accidentally turn it away. Make a preliminary cut with the deep-fluted gouge at the chalk mark to prevent ripping the bark off the rim area (cut C; Fig 9.6). The rest of the log can then be

Fig 9.4 Mounting the log between centres

Fig 9.5 Trimming the ends of the log (cuts A and B)

Fig 9.6 Cut C serves to part off the area (to the left of the white chalk mark) in which the bark will be retained

Fig 9.7 Using the spindle roughing gouge to trim the rest of the log to a cylinder (cut D)

Fig 9.9 Using the deep-fluted gouge to form the dovetail spigot

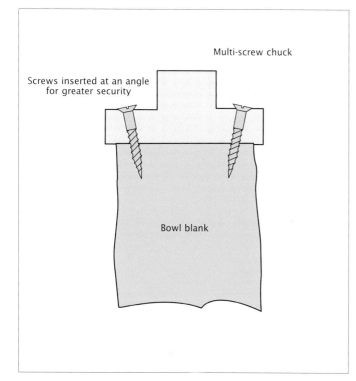

Multi-screw chuck

Screws inserted at an angle for greater security

Bowl blank

Fig 9.8 Mounting the end-grain blank on a multi-screw chuck (faceplate)

trimmed lightly with the spindle roughing gouge (cut D; Fig 9.7).

Prepare the base end for the next holding method by making a spigot. (If you prefer to make a flat surface for a faceplate instead, don't forget to mark pencil lines as described for the previous project (pages 84–5)). If you are using a multi-screw chuck, as shown in the drawings for this project, and the screws are close to the edge of the log, put them in at an angle to give a stronger grip and prevent breakout (Fig 9.8). As the photographs show, I prefer to use a spigot chuck for these small bowls, as this makes it easier to remount the blank accurately (Figs 9.9 and 9.10).

Fig 9.10 The dovetail spigot mounted in the O'Donnell jaws

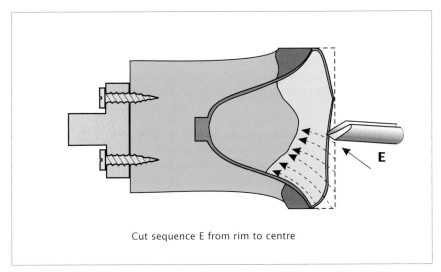

Cut sequence E from rim to centre

Fig 9.11 Natural-edge end-grain bowl: first stage of hollowing

Fig 9.12 Before beginning cut sequence E, the pip left by the tailstock centre is removed

Fig 9.13 Hollowing in progress (cut sequence E)

4 Turning the inside

On a natural-edge bowl of this shape, do the inside first. With the blank mounted in either of the two ways just described, remove the tailstock or swivel the headstock, as appropriate; then you are ready to start hollowing out the inside. With a natural-edge bowl there are two stages to this. The first is to shape the rim, which is worked towards the centre with a deep-fluted gouge (cut sequence E in Fig 9.11, and Figs 9.12–9.14), making each cut follow the finished shape. This cut is against the grain, but if the tool is

Fig 9.14 The rounded boss left in the centre of the bowl on completion of cut sequence E

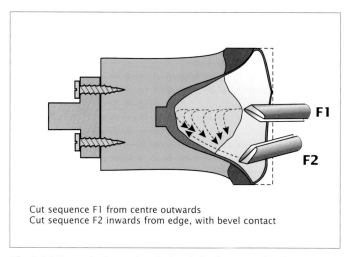

Cut sequence F1 from centre outwards
Cut sequence F2 inwards from edge, with bevel contact

Fig 9.15 Natural-edge end-grain bowl: final stages of hollowing

Fig 9.16 Hollowing nearing completion (cut sequence F)

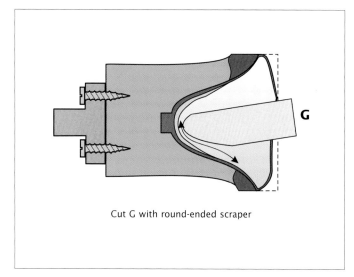

Cut G with round-ended scraper

Fig 9.17 Natural-edge end-grain bowl: finishing the inside

Fig 9.18 Smoothing the inside with the round-ended scraper (cut G)

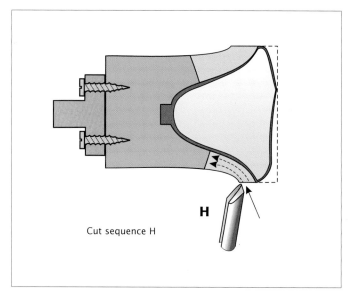

Cut sequence H

Fig 9.19 Natural-edge end-grain bowl: shaping the outside of the rim

sharp and the wood in good condition then the finish will be good. For very shallow bowls, this cut can be used for all the hollowing out. Don't forget to use a piece of white plastic or card behind the work, as before, to help make the intermittent edge more visible.

The remainder of the inside is also hollowed out with the deep-fluted gouge, working from the centre outwards (cut sequence F1 in Fig 9.15), pivoting the tool in the support hand, which is firmly on the rest. Although we are cutting with the grain, form control is limited because there is no bevel contact, so cut F2, with bevel contact, is needed to refine the shape (Fig 9.16). Final shaping is done with the large, round left-hand side-cut scraper (cut G in Fig 9.17, and Fig 9.18). This is also used to blend in the bowl to the rim area – but remember to exercise extreme care when approaching the natural bark rim.

The inside is now ready for sanding; but it is wet, and we want it to remain wet while the outside is turned, which brings us to the pleasures of wet sanding. The abrasive should be fabric-backed, and made with a resin-based adhesive so that it can withstand the wetting. With a bucket of water handy, the inside can be hand-sanded and the water used to remove the sludge at regular intervals. I find this a very pleasurable process, as there is no dust, and in the winter I use warm water. **Again, do not use this method if there is any danger of water coming into contact with the electrics of the lathe.**

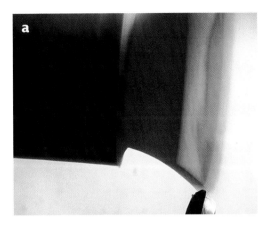

Fig 9.20 Shaping the rim (cut sequence H). A light placed behind allows the wall thickness to be seen in the area where the rim is intermittent, and gives a guide to wood thickness elsewhere

5 Turning the outside

The deep-fluted gouge is also used for the outside. Shining a light inside the bowl will give you a visual guide to the thickness. Tackle the rim first (cut sequence H in Fig 9.19, and Fig 9.20), and proceed down the bowl to the base in stages, as for the previous project (cut sequences J–L; Figs 9.21–9.25). Sand each section as it is finished.

6 Parting off

Parting off with a shallow-fluted gouge will allow you to undercut the base slightly, giving the bowl a stable stance (cut N and Fig 9.26). Sand the base by hand.

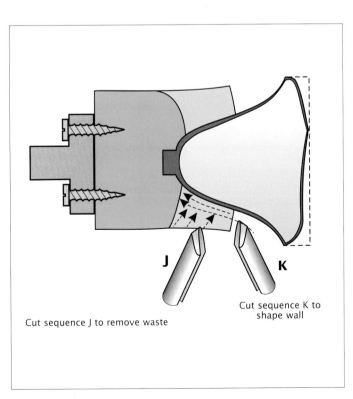

Cut sequence J to remove waste

Cut sequence K to shape wall

Fig 9.21 Natural-edge end-grain bowl: shaping the outside of the bowl wall

Fig 9.22 Forming the lower part of the bowl wall: (*a*) removing the waste (cut sequence J); (*b*) shaping the wall (cut sequence K). The light behind gives an indication of thickness

7 Drying

Dry over 2–3 days in cool conditions.

8 Applying finish

Apply the finish of your choice as described on page 43.

Fig 9.23 Natural-edge end-grain bowl: final cuts

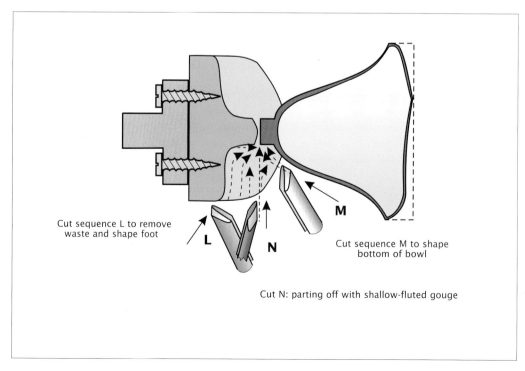

Cut sequence L to remove waste and shape foot

L

N

M

Cut sequence M to shape bottom of bowl

Cut N: parting off with shallow-fluted gouge

Fig 9.24 Removing waste from the foot area (cut sequence L)

Fig 9.25 Shaping the foot by cutting alternately (*a*) along and (*b*) towards the foot (cut sequences L and M)

Fig 9.26 Parting off with the shallow-fluted gouge, which enables the base to be slightly undercut at the same time

10 Natural-edge end-grain goblet

The natural-edge end-grain goblet is an extension of the natural-edge end-grain bowl and is an interesting exercise, challenging the skill and delicacy of the turner. The end product can be an exquisite piece (Fig 10.1).

1 Design

Fig 10.2 shows a simple design which keeps technical difficulties to a minimum and yet is very elegant. It is easy enough to hold on a 2in (51mm) spigot, but is too small for a multi-screw chuck.

2 Planning the process

1 Mark out the blank length on the timber.
2 Cut the blank from the log with a bush saw or bandsaw.
3 Mark the centres on each end of the log.
4 Rough out between centres to balance the blank and prepare it for the second holding on a 2in (51mm) spigot chuck.

Fig 10.1 Thin-stemmed goblets like this are amongst the more spectacular products of green turning

5 Turn the inside, holding in the spigot chuck; sand when finished.

6 Turn the outside of the bowl, with light shining through; sand when finished.

7 Turn the stem, supporting the bowl with revolving centre and tissue paper. Complete turning, sanding at each stage. Parting off will not be required.

8 Dry the piece for 24 hours in cool conditions.

9 Apply finish.

3 Sizing the blank

The base needs to be undercut to give an even wall thickness. This will be done with the shallow-fluted gouge, so we need plenty of access space between the foot and the chuck jaws – about 2in (50mm) will be adequate. Fig 10.3 shows the goblet with all the necessary allowances, which give a blank length of 8¾in (220mm). Some support will be

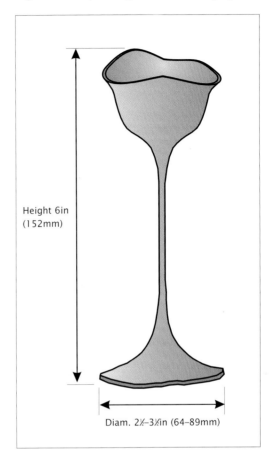

Fig 10.2 A simple design for a natural-edge goblet

Height 6in (152mm)

Diam. 2½–3½in (64–89mm)

Fig 10.3 Sizing the blank for the natural-edge goblet

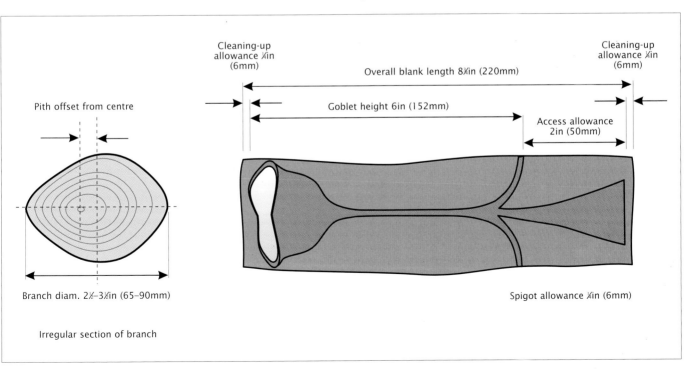

Cleaning-up allowance ¼in (6mm)

Cleaning-up allowance ¼in (6mm)

Overall blank length 8¾in (220mm)

Pith offset from centre

Goblet height 6in (152mm)

Access allowance 2in (50mm)

Branch diam. 2½–3½in (65–90mm)

Spigot allowance ¼in (6mm)

Irregular section of branch

given to the bowl end of the goblet while the stem is turned.

Fig 10.4 The material requirements for this piece are quite modest. Any branch or leaning trunk is likely to contain reaction wood, and therefore to have an off-centre pith, which is important for the stem of the goblet

Fig 10.5 The blank cut to length, with the goblet centre and the pith of the branch marked on the end; the two marks must not coincide

4 Material selection

Selecting the right branch is the next step (Fig 10.4). What we are looking for is a close-grained wood, translucent, with a thin bark, which should be in a fresh condition. It should be irregular in section so as to give an interesting rim shape. The pith, which is the weakest part of the branch, should be off-centre (see 'Reaction wood' on pages 6–7) so that it will not run through the thin stem of the goblet. There should be no branches or knots, as these are liable to run through the stem and weaken it. If in doubt, throw it out and choose another.

5 Making the piece

1 Marking out the blank

Mark the position of the blank on the log with chalk.

2 Cutting the blank

Cut the log to length with bush saw or bandsaw, taking great care not to damage the bark.

3 Marking the centres

Mark the physical centre on both ends, then look at the pith positions in relation to the centre marks at both ends (Fig 10.5). A ¼in (6mm) separation between pith and centre is comfortable; ⅛in (3mm) is a little close, but may be all right providing the two lines don't come any closer, or cross at some point in the wood; Fig 10.6 shows some examples of pieces which should be discarded. A good check is to look at one end and hold the branch so that the pith is

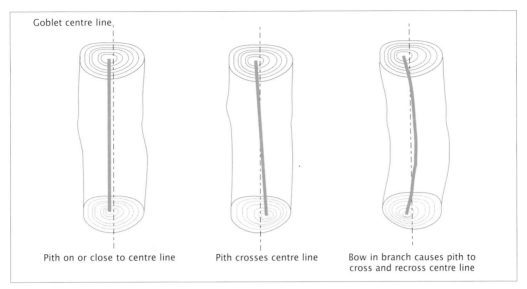

Goblet centre line

Pith on or close to centre line

Pith crosses centre line

Bow in branch causes pith to cross and recross centre line

Fig 10.6 Blank selection for the natural-edge goblet: situations to avoid

on the left and the centre is on the right. Then flip the piece end over end towards you so that you are looking at the other end: if the positions of the pith and centre are the same you are OK, but if they are different at all you will have to make a judgement on how close their paths come. A bend in the branch in the direction of the pith will increase the distance between the central axis and the pith – but it will also result in the grain running diagonally across the stem, which will weaken it. Being methodical and anticipating problems when turning is a great asset: it

makes the process easier as you make more of the same pieces.

Select which is to be the top and bottom of the piece, and mark them so that if you put the blank down and pick it up again you will not have to repeat this decision.

4 Roughing out

The first stage entails holding between centres, with the top of the blank at the headstock end (Fig 10.7). Hold it lightly between the points, so that you can spin

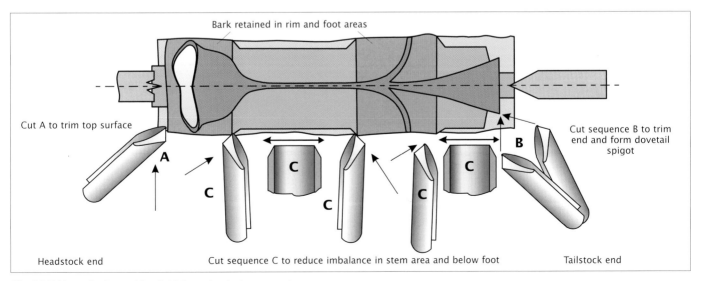

Bark retained in rim and foot areas

Cut A to trim top surface

Cut sequence B to trim end and form dovetail spigot

A

B

C

C

C

C

C

Headstock end

Cut sequence C to reduce imbalance in stem area and below foot

Tailstock end

Fig 10.7 Natural-edge goblet: initial turning between centres

Fig 10.8 The goblet blank mounted between centres, with chalk marks indicating the rim and foot areas in which the bark must be retained

Fig 10.9 Forming the dovetail spigot by cutting alternately (*a*) from the side and (*b*) from the end of the blank (cut sequence B)

Fig 10.10 Reducing the imbalance in the waste areas by (*a*) setting in with the deep-fluted gouge on the chalk marks and (*b*) making short planing cuts with the spindle roughing gouge (cut sequence C)

Fig 10.11 The piece remounted in the O'Donnell jaws, using the dovetail spigot. The rim and foot areas of the blank are still completely untouched

Fig 10.12 The first step after remounting is to remove the pip left by the tailstock centre

the wood easily to check the alignment of the rim and base; make any adjustments necessary. Keep an eye on the pith position. Then tighten up the tailstock. Using chalk, mark on the blank two bands about 1in (25mm) wide, within which the rim and base are going to be (Fig 10.8). This is to help you visualize where the goblet lies within the piece of wood, and avoid the mistake of removing the bark from these areas during the initial stages.

True up both ends and make a 2in (51mm) spigot at the base end to suit the chuck (Fig 10.9). Then, taking care, reduce the imbalance in the areas outside the chalk lines. Make the initial cuts on the chalk lines with the deep-fluted gouge, then roughly round between these cuts with the spindle roughing gouge (Fig 10.10). Take off the minimum necessary, so as to avoid cutting into the bowl of the goblet and to maintain maximum strength for the turning. The piece is now ready to be remounted in the spigot chuck (Fig 10.11).

5 Turning the inside

This stage follows exactly the same procedure as for the natural-edge end-grain bowl, including the sanding (Figs 10.12–10.16; compare pages 97–9

a

b

Fig 10.13 Hollowing in progress, cutting from rim to centre (cf. cut sequence E in Figs 9.11 and 9.13)

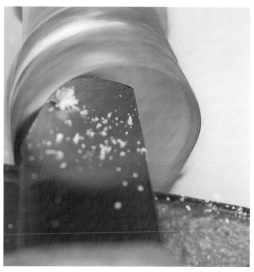

Fig 10.14 The cone of waste wood left in the centre on completion of cut sequence E

and Figs 9.11–9.18, cuts E–G). Once turning has started, the wood will begin to lose moisture by evaporation, and it may be advisable to retard the moisture loss by watering the wood as you work (Fig 10.17). **This must not be done if there is any danger of water coming into contact with the electrics of the lathe.**

Fig 10.16 Cleaning up the inside with the round-ended scraper (cf. cut G in Figs 9.17 and 9.18); this stage is followed by sanding

6 Turning the outside of the bowl

This is also the same as for the natural-edge end-grained bowl, up to the point where you have reached about ¾in

Fig 10.15 Final cut to inside with gouge (cf. cut F2 in Fig 9.15)

Fig 10.17 Watering the work to retard moisture loss; **do this only if it is safe to do so on your particular lathe**

Fig 10.18 First stage of shaping the outside (cf. cut sequences H–K in Figs 9.19–9.22). Use a light to help gauge the thickness, as before, and sand each section as it is complete

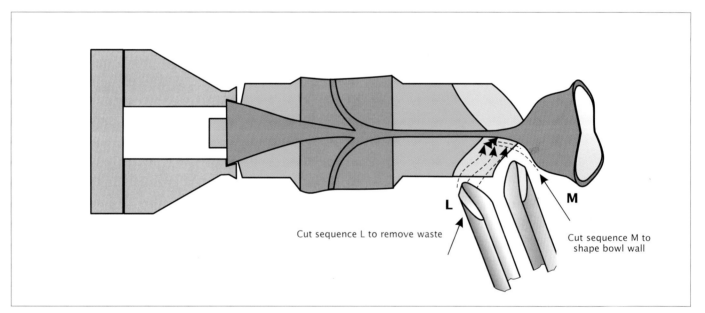

Cut sequence L to remove waste

L

M

Cut sequence M to shape bowl wall

Fig 10.19 Natural-edge goblet: transition from bowl to stem

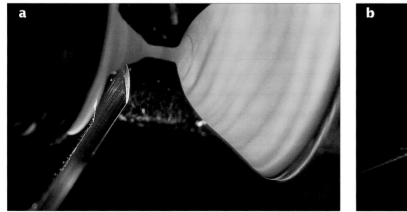

Fig 10.20 Making the transition from bowl to stem: (*a*) removing the waste (cut sequence L); (*b*) shaping the bowl wall (cut sequence M)

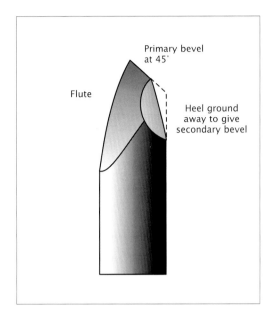

Fig 10.21 Deep-fluted gouge modified to improve clearance

Primary bevel at 45°

Flute

Heel ground away to give secondary bevel

Fig 10.22 Packing the bowl with tissue paper before bringing up the tailstock for support

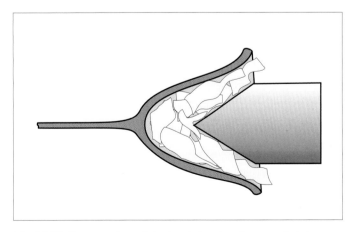

Fig 10.23 Cutaway view of the bowl showing the crumpled tissue paper surrounding the revolving centre

(20mm) diameter on the outside, at the base of the bowl (Fig 10.18; compare pages 98–100 and Figs 9.19–9.22, cuts H–K). At this point the bowl is finished, and we now proceed with the stem.

7 Turning the stem

This is done in stages, about ½–¾in (13–20mm) at a time. Each stage consists of three steps: clearing space from the base side, then turning the finished shape towards the base, and finally sanding.

The first section is the trickiest, getting round the corner from the bowl to the stem (cuts L and M in Fig 10.19, and Fig 10.20). I continue to use the deep-fluted gouge for this, but there are two methods to make it easier. The first is to grind away the heel of the bevel, thus reducing the length of the primary bevel, which will make it easier to turn the corner in the confined space (Fig 10.21). The second is to raise the tip of the tool so that it is pointing above the lathe axis; this means that, as the bowl is finished and the stem is reached, the cutting action moves from the tip of the gouge to the bottom long edge, which slides along the stem. The second method is easier and carries less risk.

Once the transition between the bowl and the stem is done, we no longer need the light shining into the bowl, so we can take it away and give the bowl some support. This will be needed as the stem gets longer, to stop the bowl whipping from side to side. The support needs to be provided without putting any pressure on the stem, which would cause it to bend. Take a small piece of tissue paper, about 6in (150mm) square – the firmer the better – crumple it into a soft ball with a depression in the middle, and put it in the bowl. Bring the tailstock with a revolving centre in it up to the depression in the tissue (Figs 10.22 and 10.23). Switch on the machine, then tighten up the tailstock until the revolving centre turns continuously. It will be necessary to

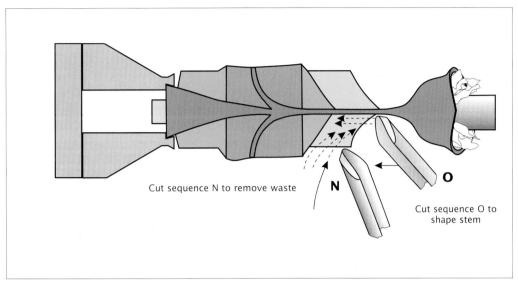

Fig 10.24 Natural-edge goblet: forming the stem

Fig 10.25 Each section of the stem is made in three stages: (*a*) removing the waste (cut sequence N); (*b*) shaping the stem (cut sequence O); (*c*) sanding

repeat the tightening from time to time, as the tissue paper will crush slightly as work proceeds.

The deep-fluted gouge will complete the turning of the stem (Figs 10.24–10.28). The clearance cuts are made towards the base, and it is a good idea to make these cuts the shape you want the base to be, so that when you come to it (cuts P and Q in Fig 10.27), the base shape occurs naturally and you only need to blend it into the stem. Remember to sand at each stage.

We need to give some thought to the underside of the base, as this affects how the goblet will stand. If it follows the top surface right from the edge, then the goblet will stand on the edge of the

Fig 10.26 The last three stages are repeated as necessary until the stem reaches the intended length

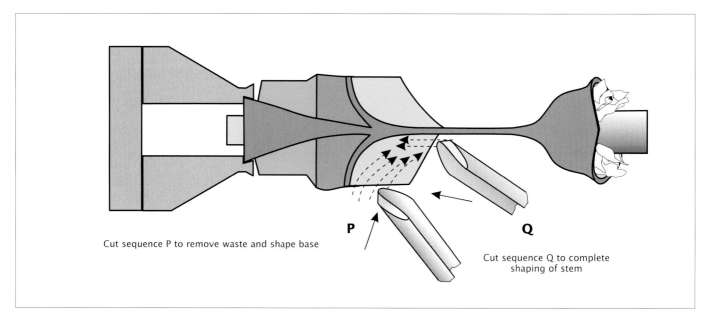

Cut sequence P to remove waste and shape base

P

Q

Cut sequence Q to complete
shaping of stem

Fig 10.27 Natural-edge goblet: forming the base

Fig 10.28 The final clearance cuts (sequence P) also serve to shape the top surface of the base (*a*), which is then blended into the stem and finally sanded (*b*)

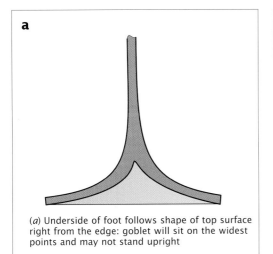

(a) Underside of foot follows shape of top surface right from the edge: goblet will sit on the widest points and may not stand upright

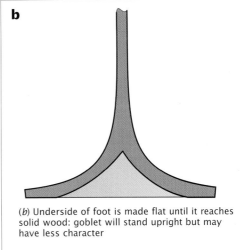

(b) Underside of foot is made flat until it reaches solid wood: goblet will stand upright but may have less character

Fig 10.29 Alternative treatments for the underside of the base

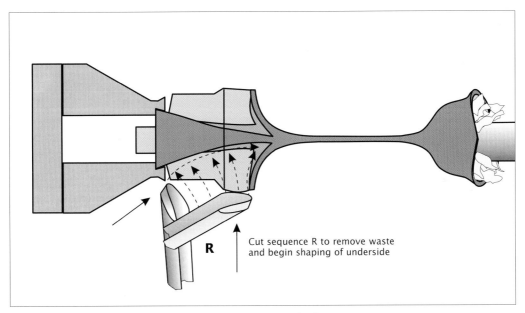

R   Cut sequence R to remove waste and begin shaping of underside

Fig 10.30 Natural-edge goblet: first stage of undercutting the foot

widest point, and because the base is not round it may not stand upright (Fig 10.29*a*). That can be an attractive design feature, but if you do want it to stand upright then the underside of the base should be flat to the point where it reaches solid wood; it can then follow the upper shape from there (Fig 10.29*b*). My preference is to follow the shape right from the edge, as this gives the pieces more individual character.

Clearing away the waste again with the deep-fluted gouge is the first step in shaping the underside, and this continues to the finish cut at the edge of the base (cut sequence R in Fig 10.30, and Fig 10.31). Do as much work as possible with the deep-fluted gouge, clearing a bit and finishing a bit, at least until you are into solid wood. As you get deeper you will notice that the headstock, the chuck and the wood will limit how far the deep-fluted gouge can be

Fig 10.31 First stage of undercutting the foot: cutting in from the edge to remove the waste (cut sequence R)

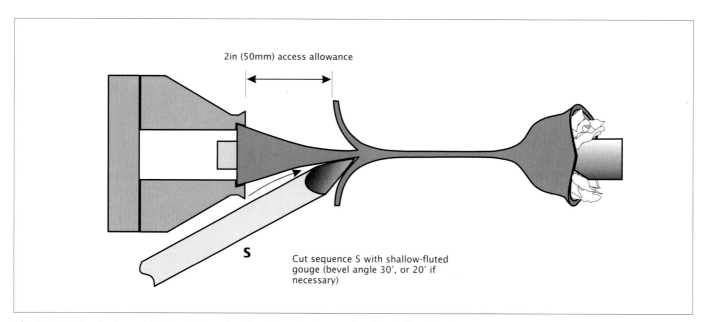

2in (50mm) access allowance

S

Cut sequence S with shallow-fluted gouge (bevel angle 30°, or 20° if necessary)

Fig 10.32 Natural-edge goblet: final stage of undercutting the foot, using the shallow-fluted gouge

a

b

c

Fig 10.33 Final stage of undercutting the foot: the cone of waste wood is pared away with the shallow-fluted gouge until it breaks away

swung around to get under the base. It is now necessary to change to a tool with a finer bevel angle and a reduced profile angle; the shallow-fluted gouge with a 30° bevel angle and a 45° profile angle is ideal. Continue as before, alternately creating space and making finishing cuts following the top shape (cut sequence S in Fig 10.32, and Fig 10.33). At the final stage even the 30° shallow-fluted gouge may need to be changed for another with a 20° bevel angle. Whichever you use, proceed with care to the eventual parting off. There will be no need to catch the goblet, as it will hang on the remaining cone of waste wood, supported by the tailstock (Fig 10.33c), bringing a great sense of relief. I don't usually sand underneath, but if you want to, you should do this at intervals as the cut progresses.

8 Drying

Being thin and even in thickness, it is unlikely that there will be any splitting problems providing the goblet is dried slowly for 24 hours in cool conditions.

9 Applying finish

My wife Liz usually colours these pieces with a water-based fabric dye (Fig 10.34); then I spray on a hard finish, which makes them easy to clean.

Fig 10.34 Completed goblets finished with fabric dye by Liz O'Donnell (photograph: Tony Boase)

11 Part-turned functional bowl

The purpose of using the part-turning process is to produce regular round vessels using the combined advantages of turning green and turning dry.

The part-turning process involves:

1 roughing out the bowl while the timber is green, leaving it oversize;
2 drying it to the required moisture content, allowing the shrinkage and distortion to take place; then
3 remounting the bowl and finishing the turning on the dry blank.

1 Design

This is to be a cross-grain functional bowl, 6¼in diameter by 2¾in high (160 x 70mm), with a maximum thickness of ½in (13mm) at the rim and a body thickness of ⅜in (10mm), as shown in Fig 11.1. Suitable woods include ash, elm, sycamore, oak, etc. (see pages 51–2). The finish will be an edible oil: either a cooking oil that will not go rancid, or liquid paraffin (mineral oil), which is a medicine for slow internal workings.

Fig 11.1 A functional bowl, made by the part-turning method so as to retain its circular shape when dry

2 Planning the process

1 Mark out the blank on the end of the log, cut a slice from the log and slab the blank to the required thickness.
2 Draw the circle on the slab and cut it out with the bandsaw.
3 Turn the outside shape: holding the blank on the top face with a 3in (76mm) faceplate and 4 screws, turn the outside 10% oversize and prepare the base for the second mounting.
4 Turn the inside shape: hold on the base with the 3in (76mm) faceplate and 4 screws in line along the grain, and turn the inside to complete stage 1.
5 Dry the bowl in the microwave.
6 Remount the dry bowl on the same faceplate in the original screw holes.
7 Finish turning both inside and outside, holding on the base.
8 Power-sand and apply finish on the lathe.
9 Part off and remount, holding on the rim, to finish the base.
10 Apply finish.

3 Sizing the blank

As with all the previous bowls, we need allowances for shrinkage, cleaning up, chucking and access, etc.; but with the part-turned bowl we also need a second cleaning-up allowance for when it is remounted after drying (see table, below left). These allowances can be kept to a minimum by selecting the orientation of the bowl blank in the tree so as to give minimal distortion (unless a particular grain pattern is required). Of the bowls shown on pages 13–14, bowl C is the one with the least distortion.

4 Material selection

Ideally, the blank should be from a straight section of the trunk so as to minimize distortion.

5 Making the piece

The general turning technique is much the same as for the other cross-grain bowls, but this time we will be using different chucking, drying and sanding methods.

1 Marking out and slabbing the blank

Draw the bowl on the end of the log to give the grain pattern required (see above and pages 12–15), cut the log to length, 1in (25mm) longer than the blank, and slab with the chainsaw (Fig 11.2).

2 Cutting out the blank

Draw a circle of the required diameter on the top of the slab, cut this out with the bandsaw and fix the faceplate on the top

	Diameter		Height	
	in	mm	in	mm
Bowl size	6¼	160	2¾	70
Shrinkage allowance, 8–10%	¾	18	¼	6
Cleaning-up allowance for both first and second turnings:				
Sides	½	12		
Top			⅜	9
Bottom			⅜	9
Parting-off allowance			¼	6
Access allowance			0	0
Chucking allowance			1	25
TOTAL	7½	190	5	125

Fig 11.2 The chainsawn slab, with the bowl and all the necessary allowances marked on the end grain

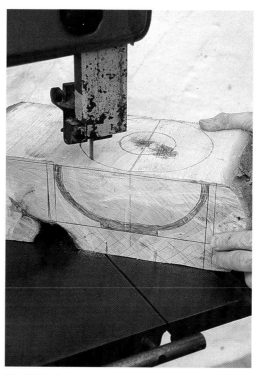

Fig 11.3 Cutting the circular blank on the bandsaw

Fig 11.4 Mounting the blank on the faceplate

Fig 11.5 Part-turned bowl: rough-turning the outside

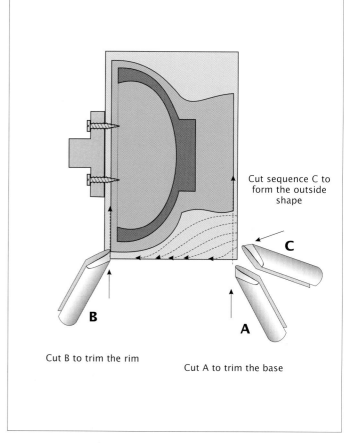

Cut sequence C to form the outside shape

C

B

A

Cut B to trim the rim

Cut A to trim the base

Fig 11.6 Trimming the base to take the faceplate for the second holding (cut A)

of the blank ready for turning (Figs 11.3 and 11.4). Using a power screwdriver with hexagon-headed screws is a quick and efficient method of mounting the bowl blank. They should penetrate ¾in (19mm) into the blank; ½in (13mm) is the minimum.

3 Turning the outside

Trim up the base ready to take the faceplate for the second holding, not forgetting the pencil lines for centring the faceplate, as before (cut A in Fig 11.5, and Fig 11.6). Turn the outside to shape with the ½in (13mm) deep-fluted gouge, following the bowl shape from the first cut (cut sequence C; Fig 11.7). If you are doing this on a long-bed lathe with a fixed head, standing on the other side of the lathe gives you the freedom to swing the tool and stay out of the way of the wood shavings. Remove the faceplate.

Fig 11.7 Stages in rough-shaping the outside, using the deep-fluted gouge (cut sequence C). Concentric rings pencilled on the base assist in locating the faceplate for the second holding

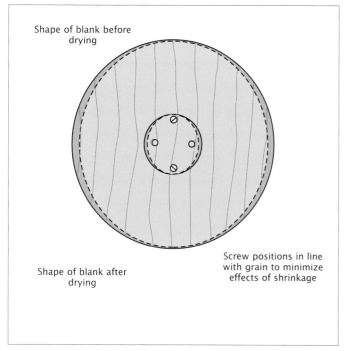

Shape of blank before drying

Shape of blank after drying

Screw positions in line with grain to minimize effects of shrinkage

Fig 11.8 Recommended screw positions for mounting the faceplate on the base of the blank

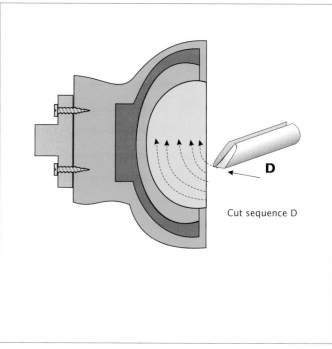

D

Cut sequence D

Fig 11.9 Part-turned bowl: rough-turning the inside

4 Turning the inside

When fixing the faceplate on the bowl base, line up the screw holes with the grain as in Fig 11.8; this will ensure that at least two of the screws will fix in the original holes after drying, as the shrinkage along the grain is negligible. As we are using a small, 3in (76mm) faceplate, all the screws should go back in the original holes.

Turn the inside of the bowl with the ½in (13mm) deep-fluted gouge, leaving the wall 1½in (38mm) thick; this amount is necessary to allow for truing the shape after the bowl has dried oval. Figs 11.9–11.11 show the turning process on the second holding.

5 Drying

For fast results, dry the bowl in the microwave, taking great care not to overheat it (see pages 27–8). Cool it as much as possible between microwave sessions, and weigh it each time. Plotting a graph of time against weight (see Fig 2.26 on page 27) will tell you when the first stage of the process is complete. Avoid overdrying. The moisture content could be checked with a moisture meter, providing you don't stick the probes in too far. This is

Fig 11.10 Truing the top surface, after remounting with the faceplate on the base of the bowl blank

Fig 11.11 Rough-turning the inside with the deep-fluted gouge (cut sequence D); the pencil mark indicates the extent of the hollowing at this stage

Fig 11.12 Part-turned bowl: second stage of turning, after drying in the microwave

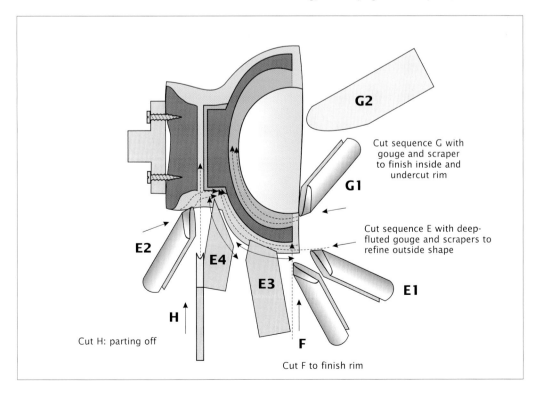

G2

Cut sequence G with gouge and scraper to finish inside and undercut rim

G1

Cut sequence E with deep-fluted gouge and scrapers to refine outside shape

E2

E4

E3

E1

H

Cut H: parting off

F

Cut F to finish rim

Fig 11.13 Refining the outside profile with the deep-fluted gouge, after drying (cut sequence E)

Fig 11.14 Sheer-scraping the outside, using (*a*) the square-ended scraper in the rim area and (*b*) the skew scraper on the part which recedes towards the foot

only likely to give you a measure of the *surface* moisture content, but with microwave drying it should be the same throughout. The drying process could take up to 24 hours.

6 Remounting for finish-turning

Reattach the faceplate by putting in two screws along the grain first, but do not tighten them yet. It should be possible to locate the other two screws in the original holes next. If not, make two more holes. As the base will not be flat, there will be gaps between the base and the faceplate on two sides; care should be taken to keep these even as the screws are tightened.

7 Finish-turning inside and outside

True up and finish the outside shape, cutting from the rim to the base with the deep-fluted gouge, then refine the shape with the large scrapers (Figs 11.12–11.14). I found the microwaved sycamore turned very nicely. Trim the rim with the deep-fluted gouge (Fig 11.15), then give it a final skim with a large scraper. Leave the

Fig 11.15 Finishing the rim with the deep-fluted gouge (cut F)

Fig 11.16 Stages in finish-turning the inside with the deep-fluted gouge (cut sequence G)

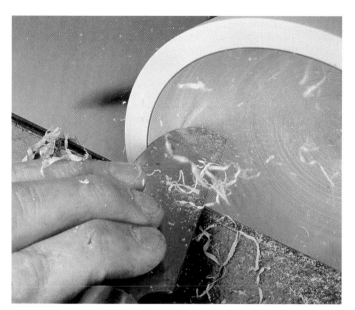

Fig 11.17 Finishing the inside with the round-ended scraper (last stage of cut sequence G); finger support may be needed near the rim

Fig 11.18 Power-sanding is a suitable technique for a bowl of this kind; do the inside first

rim ½in (13mm) wide, then undercut it to give a wall thickness of ⅜in (10mm); this gives a very nice feel to the bowl. Turn the inside to a finish with the deep-fluted gouge (Fig 11.16); also use a large scraper as necessary (Fig 11.17).

8 Sanding and finishing

Sand the bowl all over. This is a suitable project on which to try power sanding (see page 43), which will quickly smooth out any irregularities and give a good surface. Use a 3in (76mm) pad with a 100-grit disc, set the toolrest to give support to the forearm, and don't forget to put on the face mask and switch on the dust extractor.

Do the inside first (Fig 11.18). Keep the disc moving, and take care to keep the edge crisp as you come up under the rim. Do the top of the rim at the same time. Follow with 180-grit pads, then 240-grit, which will give a very smooth surface.

Repeat the process on the outside, but tuck your elbows in to your sides for stability and move your body to follow the bowl shape (Fig 11.19). Don't worry about reaching right down to the foot at this stage. If you kept good control over the sanding, both edges of

Fig 11.19 To sand the outside, keep your elbows tucked in for stability

the rim will be very sharp, and you will need to touch them lightly with a fine piece of sandpaper.

The oil finish can now be applied and buffed in the lathe. Allow to dry between coats, and again before taking the bowl off the lathe.

9 Parting off and finishing the base

Part off with the narrow fluted parting tool (Fig 11.20).

Remount the bowl, using the contracting wooden jaws on the scroll chuck (Figs 11.21 and 11.22). This gives good access to finish around the base and slightly hollow underneath (Fig 11.23).

Fig 11.20 Parting off (cut H), with right hand ready to catch the bowl

Fig 11.21 Part-turned bowl: finishing the base in the wooden jaws

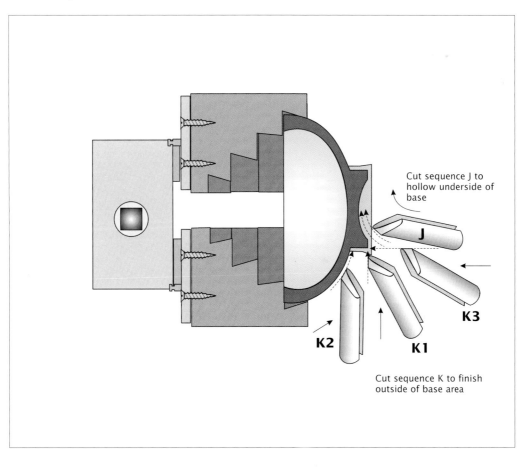

Cut sequence J to hollow underside of base

J

K2

K1

K3

Cut sequence K to finish outside of base area

Fig 11.22 Remounting the bowl in the contracting wooden jaws

Fig 11.23 Finishing the base with a slight hollow underneath (cut sequence J), prior to finishing the outside of the foot (sequence K)

The underside of the base could be power-sanded, but the side of the base and the lower part of the bowl adjacent to it should be hand-sanded using the same abrasive as was used for the power-sanding.

10 Applying finish

To complete the bowl, apply the oil finish as before.

Photograph: Glyn Satterley

Select bibliography

Abbott, Mike, *Green Woodwork* (Lewes: GMC Publications, 1989).

Bramwell, Martyn (ed.), *The International Book of Wood* (London: Mitchell Beazley, 1976)

Brown, W. H., *Timbers of the World*, 7: *North America* (London: Timber Research and Development Association, 1978)

——*Timbers of the World*, 8: *Australasia* (London: Timber Research and Development Association, 1978)

Handbook of Hardwoods (London: Dept of the Environment, 1972; 5th edn., rev. by R. H. Farmer, 1988)

Handbook of Softwoods (London: Dept of the Environment, 1977; 4th edn., 1986)

Hoadley, R. Bruce, *Understanding Wood* (Newtown, CT: Taunton, 1980)

Lavers, Gwendoline M., *The Strength and Properties of Timber* (London: Dept of the Environment, 1967; 3rd edn., rev. by G. L. Moore, 1983)

Walker, Aidan (gen. ed.), *The Encyclopedia of Wood* (London: Quarto, 1989)

Metric conversion table

inches to millimetres

in	mm		in	mm		in	mm
⅛	3		9	229		30	762
¼	6		10	254		31	787
⅜	10		11	279		32	813
½	13		12	305		33	838
⅝	16		13	330		34	864
¾	19		14	356		35	889
⅞	22		15	381		36	914
1	25		16	406		37	940
1¼	32		17	432		38	965
1½	38		18	457		39	991
1¾	44		19	483		40	1016
2	51		20	508		41	1041
2½	64		21	533		42	1067
3	76		22	559		43	1092
3½	89		23	584		44	1118
4	102		24	610		45	1143
4½	114		25	635		46	1168
5	127		26	660		47	1194
6	152		27	686		48	1219
7	178		28	711		49	1245
8	203		29	737		50	1270

About the author

After a career which began in engineering, including a spell as a research and development engineer in the nuclear industry, Michael, his wife Liz and children Cullen and Joanne took to the crofting life on Dunnet Head, the most northerly point on the Scottish mainland. Although Caithness is a windswept, treeless landscape (well, almost), it became the basis for a new career in woodturning which has led to exhibiting and teaching around the world.

Index